Critical Guides to German Texts

D0223849

7 Goethe: Faust I

Critical Guides to German Texts

EDITED BY MARTIN SWALES

GOETHE

Faust I

Michael Beddow

Professor of German
University of Leeds

Grant & Cutler Ltd
1986

© Grant & Cutler Ltd
1986

Library of Congress Cataloging-in-Publication Data

Beddow, Michael.
  Goethe, Faust I.

  (Critical guides to German texts; 7)
  Bibliography: p.
  1. Goethe, Johann Wolfgang von, 1749-1832. Faust. 1.
Theil. I. Title. II. Series.
PT1925.B37 1986   832'.6   86-22876
ISBN 0-7293-0261-X

I.S.B.N. 84-599-1868-8

DEPÓSITO LEGAL: V. 96 - 1987

Printed in Spain by
Artes Gráficas Soler, S.A., Valencia
for
GRANT & CUTLER LTD
55-57, GREAT MARLBOROUGH STREET, LONDON W1V 2AY
and
27, SOUTH MAIN STREET, WOLFEBORO, NH 03894-2069, USA

Contents

Preface

Any study of *Faust I* must be too short for its subject matter: the problem is which essentials to dispense with. Writing for someone who has read through the work at least once before approaching it again with this guide, I have made no attempt to survey critical opinion on all controversial points. The views I argue have been influenced by the scholarly debates, as I hope specialist readers will recognise; but there was seldom room to acknowledge that influence explicitly.

Except where absolutely necessary, facts about *Faust I* readily accessible elsewhere have not been repeated. I assume that readers will make use of, at least, the commentaries of Friedrich and Scheithauer (*23*) and of Trunz in the *Hamburger Ausgabe* (*1*). I have, however, included a very rudimentary appendix on scanning German verse, since this information is hard to come by in English. Wherever possible, references are by line number, so any edition (or even an English translation) may be used. Actual quotations cite the Reclam edition rather than the *Hamburger Ausgabe*, which scrupulously marks the many elided 'e's by apostrophes: the Reclam edition omits apostrophes where current usage allows, and the result is easier on a modern reader's eye. There is also one passage where the punctuation of the *Hamburger Ausgabe* is seriously misleading, as the commentary on *Vor dem Tor* will show.

Other references, indicated by italicised figures (as above), are to the numbered items in the Select Bibliography.

This book was written at King's College, London. My thanks are due to the participants in classes on *Faust* who posed awkward questions, and above all to my colleague Robin Harrison, whose knowledge, dedication and good humour help create a stimulating climate for eighteenth-century studies in the College and the University.

Introduction

I Faust *and the critical tradition*[1]

A survey of the enormous range of critical writing on Goethe's *Faust* suggests three things above all that any new study must cope with:

1. The play gives new meanings to key terms in the Faust story. To grasp these meanings we have to concentrate on how they take issue with the old ones. Failure to appreciate just what is old *and* new about the way notions such as good and evil are used in the play creates false difficulties and hides genuine problems of interpretation.

2. *Faust I* has existed for more than a century and a half in a culture where literary studies and the performing arts are closely bound up with ideology. The text needs disentangling from various attempts to harness it to the defence or pursuit of political power. The National Socialist view of Faust as proto-type Führer (see *33*) is easy enough to discount, as are the tedious orthodoxies of Marxist criticism. Harder to undo are the insidious distortions which generations of allegedly 'unpolitical' literary scholarship have produced. History, so that scholarly tradition claims, is a matter of vulgar events, whereas art should be occupied with eternal human values. But no one understood better than Goethe that history is not just a background to human experience, but part of its essential stuff; and that historical changes in his own age were altering conceptions of human nature faster and more radically than at any previous time. *Faust I* can only come alive for us if we grasp how it draws drama out of the spiritual, intellectual and moral dilemmas of

[1] Surveys by Atkins (*7* and *8*), by Haile (*27*, pp.158-86) and by Boyle (*12*) offer a useful, if necessarily partial, introduction to this field. For more comprehensive and up to date bibliographical information, consult the periodical *Goethe* (called since 1972 *Goethe Jahrbuch*).

the late eighteenth century, dilemmas whose consequences are still with us.

3. The issue of the play's unity has given rise to countless problems of interpretation. The difficulties stem as much from the questions that have been asked as from the answers offered. There are, in fact, two distinct but related problems. The first concerns the internal structure of *Faust I*, the second (which cannot be examined here) the relationship between Parts I and II. The structure of *Faust I* has always been considered problematic. It plainly lacks conventional divisions into acts and scenes, and the action can appear strangely jerky and laconic. In addition, the diverse origins of the raw material, partly stemming from the Faust tradition, partly very much the product of Goethe's imagination, fostered a belief that the play's unity had to be demonstrated rather than assumed. The discovery of the manuscript that became known as the *Urfaust*[2] seemed to hamper such demonstrations, since it offered a basis for treating *Faust I* in the way the 'Higher Criticism' of the Bible viewed scriptural documents: as texts whose canonical form was the result of earlier versions and meanings being overlaid and distorted by later generations of editors and compilers. Where *Faust I* contains apparent contradictions or inconsistencies, commentators in the first decades of this century tended to explain them as unintended confusions resulting from a thought-less combination of passages written at different times: the idea that such points may resist easy assimilation precisely because something new and significant is being said was not given due weight.[3] Scholars who rightly felt *Faust I* to be more than a mere rag-bag did not opt for the strongest counter-argument: a demonstration that the play, for all its unorthodox outward appearance, has an overall dramatic unity, that is a unity established by the presence of a dominant plot-line with its intrinsic conflict, climax and resolution. Instead, they mostly attempted the weaker defence of claiming that there were two

---

[2] See *35*; and for the *Entstehungsgeschichte* in general, *23*, pp.67-76.

[3] This tendency has not altogether disappeared: it is present, for example, in the chapter on *Faust* in Gray (*26*, pp.126-85).

dramas, a 'Gelehrtentragödie' and a 'Gretchentragödie', essentially disparate, but each with its own internal structure.[4] Or they discounted the importance of distinctively dramatic unity altogether, and argued that the play's essential cohesion was established by patterns of recurrent imagery, reflection and antithesis, by the alternation of movements of expansion and contraction, and through cunningly threaded leitmotifs.[5] It would be silly to deny the presence of such patterns; but I doubt whether the view of the play as a rag-bag is sufficiently plausible to justify all the ingenuity expended on countering it with non-dramatic conceptions of unity — especially when they run the risk of submerging the genuinely dramatic coherence which I shall try to demonstrate.[6]

II *The lessons of the* Entstehungsgeschichte

To explain away difficult passages as the unintentional result of the way *Faust I* was constructed is a misuse of the *Entstehungsgeschichte*. But some knowledge of the stages in which the play was written can sharpen our perception of its final import (see table). In the portions originating in 1772-75 and 1788-90, we are not shown how Mephistopheles and Faust came together, or on what terms. The fact that the *Studierzimmer* scenes are part of the very last layer in the play's creation emphasises that Goethe's interest in the Faust material had a different focus from his predecessors'. It is equally striking that Gretchen is there from the outset. Everything of substance in the portrayal of her destiny is found in the earliest

---

[4] The most recent representative of this view in its extreme form is Mason (*34*).

[5] This trend was begun by an important essay by Willoughby (*47*). For Willoughby and his more moderate successors (e.g. Atkins, *6*) the search for 'morphological' principles proceeds alongside a recognition of dramatic structures. But in Requadt (*37*), Jantz (*28*) and others, reflections, recurrent patterns and leitmotifs tend to bury any sense of dramatic tension, movement and resolution. So it is to be welcomed that the most recent attempt to argue a detailed and elaborate structure for the play, by Fowler (*22*), returns to Willoughby's respect for the play as drama.

[6] Dramatic structure is not the same thing as stageability. It may well be that Goethe thought the play beyond the resources and talents of contemporary German companies; but that does not mean he was not aiming at specifically dramatic effects.

The origins of *Faust I*: a tabular summary

This table is not meant to replace a detailed survey of the
Entstehungsgeschichte. It provides a quick reference to the
stages in the work's composition to which the material in each
scene belongs. No account is taken of changes to that material,
however substantial, from version to version. The stages in the
work's composition are indicated as follows:

I — 1772-1775   II — 1788-1790   III — 1797-1801

Name of Scene	Lines in *Faust I*	Stage of origin
Zueignung	1-32	III
Vorspiel auf dem Theater	33-242	III
Prolog im Himmel	243-353	III
Nacht	354-597	I
	598-601	III
	602-605	I
	606-807	III
Vor dem Tor	808-1177	III
Studierzimmer I	1178-1529	III
Studierzimmer II	1530-1769	III
	1770-1867	II
	1868-2050	I
	2051-2072	II
Auerbachs Keller	2073-2336	I
Hexenküche	2337-2604	II

stratum of the play. Again, we are alerted to the distinctive way Goethe sees the Faust material. From the start Gretchen, a figure without parallel in earlier versions of the Faust story,[7] is central to Goethe's conception, a fact that rules out a division of the play into a 'Gelehrtentragödie' and a 'Gretchentragödie' even before detailed analysis makes it untenable.

The *Entstehungsgeschichte* also reminds us that our text is subtitled *Der Tragödie erster Teil*. There was, in Goethe's mind, much more to come, though precisely what was by no means clear when he dispatched *Faust I* to the press. We must try to occupy the narrow, but essential, ground between seeing *Faust I* as a fully concluded play and claiming that it makes no sense without consideration of *Faust II*. Faust's career is by no means over when he flees from Gretchen's prison; but that does not mean that we can draw no conclusions about him or about the course of his life thus far portrayed. We must neither overstate nor devalue the completeness of *Faust I*.

III *The Spies* Faustbuch

There was at least one real Faust in sixteenth-century Germany.[8] But the first Faust we are concerned with was essentially the creation of an author of whom we know nothing, apart from what he did with the Faust story and why he did it. He took various tales of the wiles and escapades of magicians then circulating in Germany and attributed them all to Johann Faust. Then he composed for this loose assembly of anecdotes a beginning and an end, telling how Faust came to acquire his powers through a pact with the devil, and how in fulfilment of that pact he was finally dragged off to Hell. The result was published anonymously in Frankfurt in 1587, becoming known, after the publisher's name, as the Spies *Faustbuch*. We do not need the declaration on the title page that the book is intended

---

[7] The passing mention of a 'ziemlich schöne doch arme Magd' in the 1674 (Pfitzer) version of the *Faustbuch* only emphasises the distance between Goethe and his predecessors in this essential respect. This may have been the version Goethe read in his youth, and he certainly borrowed a copy while in the last stages of writing *Faust I*. But it hardly matters.

[8] More details in *17*.

'allen hochtragenden, fürwitzigen und gottlosen Menschen zum schrecklichen Beispiel / abscheulichen Exempel und treuherziger Warnung'[9] to see that the author's purpose was didactic. But the precise target of his religious zeal deserves closer examination.

Ritual magic, the attempt by human beings to compel spirits to do their bidding, has a long history: it is certainly far older than Christianity. With the establishment of European Christendom, ritual magic came to be seen in an increasingly sinister light.[10] The notion that the ritual magician can exercise complete control over the spirits he summons gave way to the belief that it was the spirits, now held to be part of the satanic host, who were really in command, and that anyone entering a pact with a spirit would be cheated on earth and damned in eternity. By the time the *Faustbuch* was written, ritual magic, once regarded as a legitimate, if marginal and highly dangerous activity, had become associated with the use of witchcraft to inflict suffering on enemies or rivals.[11]

But the chief polemical target of the Spies *Faustbuch* is the motive behind Faust's conclusion of a satanic pact, rather than his dealing with the devil in itself. Faust, we read, was not content to exercise his outstanding intellect within the bounds set by scriptural revelation: '[er] nahm an sich Adlers Flügel, wollte alle Gründ am Himmel und Erden erforschen' (p.8). And it is chiefly in pursuit of knowledge that Faust concludes his satanic pact. For the *Faustbuch* author, the frontiers of legitimate human knowledge are set, not by any limitations intrinsic to the human mind, but by divine decree. All that human beings need and are permitted to know about their world, their history and their destiny is in the Bible: any attempt to explore what the Bible does not reveal is a transgression against God.

[9] All quotations from the Spies *Faustbuch* are from the edition by Benz (*4*). This is not the best text to pursue a scholarly interest in the original *Faustbuch*, since the editor has deliberately incorporated some passages from later editions, and the spelling has been modernised. But it makes the *Faustbuch* readily accessible to modern readers.

[10] See *15* and *16*.

[11] For a fascinating account of this conflation and its consequences in the witch-hunts of the sixteenth century, see *18*.

The notion of a link between human curiosity and divine dis-
pleasure is, of course, very ancient. Adam and Eve were expelled
from Eden because they broke the divine command not to eat of
the Tree of Knowledge. But the *Faustbuch* is a creation of the
last quarter of the sixteenth century, an age that had seen the
voyages of discovery, the Renaissance revival of classical
scholarship and the first stirrings of what would become the new
science of nature; and when a work written in such an age tars
intellectual enquiry with the same brush as Satanism, the
familiar fear of spiritual pride has acquired a vast new
dimension: it has become a fear about the course of Western
history. The *Faustbuch* author may not consciously have
grasped that the thirst for knowledge which drives his Faust
away from respectable scholarship into the arms of the devil also
makes him embody the great historical movement of his day
towards the expansion of knowledge by secular enquiry. He may
simply have thought he was castigating the villainy of an individual into which other individuals at any time or place might
fall if not forewarned; but in fact he was fighting a rearguard
action for a view of human knowledge whose chief bastions were
already breached, and which would collapse entirely in the
following century.

IV *Secularisation*

Goethe turned to the Faust material at a time when the
changes which the *Faustbuch* author so feared had already
begun to reshape Western culture, and he was well aware of the
historical import of his undertaking. If we want a single word
for those changes, we could do worse then 'secularisation'.
Broadly speaking, secularisation is the replacement of the
traditional theological bases of political, moral and social order
by foundations requiring no supernatural sanction or special
revelation. In the latter half of the eighteenth century secularisation was causing considerable disquiet in Germany, and not
only among the adherents of traditional religious belief. This
disquiet was expressed in two dilemmas which underlie the predicament of Goethe's Faust figure.

In science, the work of Galileo, Kepler and Newton had replaced the old understanding of the physical world as a collection of individual essences, each obeying the laws of its particular God-given nature, by a view of the universe as a vast mechanism in which bodies composed of the same elementary materials interacted according to a relatively simple set of mathematically formulated laws. These laws could be understood by human beings, and in some cases manipulated by them. An enormous increase in ability to explain and control the world was the undeniable result. But the new scientists had to consider only the computible dimensions of the natural world. Mass, position and rates of motion were all that mattered: the concrete qualities of things, and personal reactions to them, had to be set aside. This threatened to dehumanise the scientist, devaluing people's spiritual, moral and emotional powers and blinding them to everything in nature that was not mathematically measurable. Did a choice have to be made between, on the one hand, the power of the new science and, on the other, the human integrity of the scientist and his living interchange with nature? This was the one of the dilemmas which exercised eighteenth-century German intellectuals.

While the new sciences were breaking down the medieval picture of how the world worked, other forces were altering the social structure of European nations, and the way that structure was understood. Forcing a complex pattern of events into a crude generalisation, one could say that the notion of a divinely ordained hierarchy of 'estates' was replaced by the idea that society was essentially a group of individuals who had come together under the institutions of civil society for their mutual benefit and protection. People came to regard themselves first and foremost as individuals and only secondarily and provisionally as members of society. At the same time, as individuals became conscious of more differentiated needs and gained the prosperity to satisfy them, an increasing specialisation and division of labour was taking place, heightening differences among individuals and widening the gap between what any one person could know or do and the total knowledge and capacities of increasingly advanced economies. The notion of a private self and a public self, the latter being an external role rather than a true self-expression, became more widespread.[12] So if the new science exalted abstract reason at the expense of other human capacities, changes in society were loosening the ties of human fellowship and replacing traditional communities by rational associations of isolated individuals. Did a choice have to be made between the new respect for individual capacities, rights and potential and the old sense of communal identity and solidarity? This was the second great dilemma seen by those in the late eighteenth century who had anxiously read the signs of the times.

These dilemmas encapsulate what a large number of thinkers in late eighteenth-century Germany regarded as the chief evils of their day: the estrangement of mankind from the natural world and hostility among human beings themselves. One common line of thought emerges among the writers, otherwise extremely diverse in outlook, who pondered such matters: these dilemmas, the product of historical change, are in one way or another to be resolved by and in history. Whether we read Kant, Herder, Schiller, Schlegel, Schelling, Fichte, Hölderlin, Kleist, Novalis or Hegel (not to mention, two generations later, Marx), we find the same thread of argument: the divisions and isolation of the present are stages in a process that has taken mankind away from intuitive interchange with nature and genuine communal living into the present age of abstraction and individualism. But that process is not yet ended: it will culminate in a new order of things where community among mankind and integration with nature is regained, without any loss of that sense of individual variety and worth which the present age has fostered.[13]

V *Theodicy, Fall and Redemption*

In every period of European culture, people have held that the world does not measure up to the highest human expectations and aspirations. In an age of faith, this sense of a discrepancy

[12] For a discussion of this change, with further references, see *43*.

[13] For numerous instances of this idea in German thinkers, and parallels with English writers of the period, see *5*.

between what is and what ought to be leads to theodicy — the attempt to show that, from a theological perspective, things that seem to be grave flaws in creation are compatible with divine goodness and omnipotence. Secularisation altered the angle from which such issues were approached. Traditional Christian theodicy argued that the evil in creation was essentially mankind's fault, not God's. God's original plan for creation had envisaged mankind in perfect happiness and harmony in an earthly paradise without death, pain or want. This plan had been thwarted by the deliberate disobedience of the first human beings, misusing the freedom of choice God had given them when making them in his own image and likeness. That primal offence corrupted the natures of Adam and Eve and all their descendants, thus explaining moral evil; and it was also held to have affected the natural world as well, engendering everything that made the world ill adapted to human aspirations and comfort. Under a secularised outlook, which resists any appeal to a creator external to the universe, such an account was unacceptable. Secular theodicies had to show that evil made sense as an intrinsic part of a larger ordered scheme, instead of being a diversion introduced by arbitrary human choices. The story of the Fall was retained as an allegory of the origins of evil; but it was re-interpreted as a parable of evolutionary development.[14] Paradise was pictured as a condition where human beings are fully at home in the natural world and live in complete harmony with one another: and evil consisted in the gap between this state and the present realities of human life. The Fall was seen, not as a consequence of a free act of disobedience which plunged the human race into a vale of misery from which only Christ's redemptive sacrifice could release them, but as an inevitable and necessary stage in the emergence of humanity. Man simultaneously emerged as man *and* entered a fallen state at the moment in evolution when he acquired what

[14] There is a widespread misconception that evolutionary views originated only in the mid-nineteenth century with Darwin and his contemporaries. On the contrary, Darwin's originality and influence lay, not in the notion of evolution itself, but in providing a purely causal account of evolutionary change, banishing from biology that concern with purposes which had been removed from physics two centuries earlier.

the eighteenth century understood by 'Vernunft'.

'Vernunft' specifies those aspects of human rationality which enable people to stand back from their immediate perceptions and experience and form notions of alternative states of affairs. It allows human beings to act freely on an awareness of alternative possibilities, rather than responding simply to the immediate situation; it lets them conceive of different conditions of existence and strive to achieve them; and it bestows reflexive self-consciousness, the ability to think about thinking and to know one is knowing. The emergence of such a faculty made the first human beings superior to their sub-human ancestors in evolutionary history; but it also made them prone to divided allegiances, conflicts of goals and ideals, and exposed them to the disabling power of excessive self-awareness. And all these things had contributed to the evil of estrangement among men and between men and nature, aggravated in more recent history by the ascendancy of analytic powers in the Enlightenment.

Identifying the Fall with the emergence of distinctively human qualities undercut Christian notions of redemption. No one can be redeemed from an essential part of the natural history of their species. Instead, redemption from this re-interpreted Fall was held to lie in the cultivation and expansion of human reason and reflexive self-consciousness until they ceased to be divisive, and yielded instead a conscious perception and recognition of the essential unity of man and nature. What had been destroyed by the development of man's distinctive consciousness was to be restored by the completion of that development. In effect, this re-interpretation of the Fall saw in the human quest for knowledge and understanding both the root cause of evil and its only true remedy. It is this vein of paradox which Goethe mines so splendidly in *Faust I*. In the *Faustbuch* there is an obvious parallel between Faust wanting to know more than the Bible reveals and the eating of the fruit from the forbidden Tree of Knowledge in Eden. The Faust story as Goethe reshapes it stands in the same relation to the new, secularised Fall myth as did the story of the *Faustbuch* Faust to the orthodox view. Goethe's Faust lives out the central tenet of the new myth: that the arduous and tortuous path to redemption is found through intensification of the original 'fault'.

It was not just a new understanding of the Fall as a necessary developmental stage that secularised redemption. To site evil and its final remedy wholly within the visible universe and the span of human history meant that redemption had ceased to be reconciliation with a God external to history and the universe (though acting through them) and become an anticipated reconciliation between human 'Vernunft' and its objects, between the subject of experience and the experienced world. To be sure, individuals were to be made whole through an encounter with something transcendent, in the sense of something greater than any one individual, but what they were to encounter was nothing more or less than the totality of creation. There was no longer an aspiration towards a creator who transcends the world itself and is, in the end, wholly distinct from it. Creation itself, rather than a divine creator, had become the object of religious awe and veneration. Divinity was seen and worshipped in two aspects of this secularised universe in particular: in the miracle of order-in-variety, persistence-in-change, which the new science could describe but not explain; and in the energy driving the universe on towards its consummation, the divine fire that shed the individual sparks of each person's urge to self-realisation. The Faustian striving, then, is more than a means to salvation: it is in itself a manifestation of divinity. The import of the *Faustbuch*, it might seem, has been completely reversed.

Yet Goethe's Faust, though a representative figure, is not an exemplary one: in an important sense, he is an evil-doer. At first sight, the secularised version of the Fall and its remedy leaves no room for evil deeds as such. Evil states of affairs, certainly; and evil attitudes, no doubt, where there is mockery of aspirations towards greater knowledge and fuller experience, or denial that the divisions and estrangement of the present are destined to be overcome — attitudes such as Mephistopheles has in plenty. But a human being genuinely striving for ever fuller experience, realising the divine potential within, might seem incapable of doing evil. That is apparently the view of Der Herr, serenely looking down and forward from Heaven; and many commentators, with greater or less enthusiasm, have claimed that the play bears him out.[15] But though the cosmic perspective established by the *Prolog im Himmel* must not be forgotten, it is not the only one from which the drama comes into focus. There is also an earthbound viewpoint, from which the pursuit of self-realisation acquires a sinister aspect, and it is from that viewpoint that Faust's treatment of Gretchen is portrayed. *Faust I* builds a drama around the moral evil engendered by the quest for fulfilment enjoined by the new secularised outlook. And it is the centrality of Gretchen, such a distinctive feature of this work from its earliest stages, which places the dramatic exploration of that moral evil at the very heart of the work and establishes its historical roots.

The action of the play resists any literal-minded 'dating': Gretchen is part of a securely pre-Reformation culture, Faust is as much a late eighteenth-century intellectual as a Renaissance magician. But this is anything but historical carelessness. History is not the representation of the past, but its interpretation. In the cause of such interpretation, Goethe concentrates a transition covering many generations into a single dramatic encounter, enacted on a stage where his imagination has projected the boundary between medieval and modern Europe.

---

[15] Most disquietingly (because of the undeniable power of the mind extolling the allegedly tragic expediency of Gretchen's destruction) in *32*, pp.128-210.

Commentary

Before the title page of *Faust I* proper, we encounter a poem and two preliminary scenes, quite diverse in manner and in their contribution to the overall work.

Zueignung

This poem belies the expectations raised by its title and placing. Dedicatory verses were commonplace in eighteenth-century works, and their matter and manner followed predictable lines. But this is no ordinary dedicatory poem. In form it uses the stanza (in the strict technical sense of the word), which Goethe liked to employ for more or less solemn reflections on his art (see *29*). And instead of the anticipated rhetorical praises of a distinguished dedicatee, we find an intense and deeply thoughtful expression of what this work means to its author.

The opening lines speak of two epochs in the poet's inner life: a remote past in which the figures of the play were once close to his youthful heart and imagination, and a present in which their insistent claims on his awareness intrude upon the clarity and rigour of his maturer years. The poet yields to the figures' persistence, won over by the atmosphere of his youth which they bring with them. The reawakening of his younger self brings more pain than joy, since it reminds him of all the former friends he has now lost, the enthusiastic soul-mates who were the infant work's first hearers. Whatever fruits his renewed labours on the play may bear will be not for them, but for a vast, unknown audience which disconcerts the poet even when it applauds his work. And yet, perhaps not. By the final stanza, the power of imagination has banished the facts of time, separation and death. It is the present that now seems remote to the poet: his new reality as he takes up the work after so many years is everything that, to prosaic eyes, seemed beyond recall.

So with that beautifully clear indirectness at which Goethe excells, the true dedicatees of what follows are identified: it is for the lost friends of his youth, vividly present to him as he resumes the work most of them will not witness in the flesh.

What a work means to its author, the way he relates to it almost as to a child of his flesh and blood, is of course a different matter from the public meanings with which literary criticism is concerned. This poem will not help us interpret the work it precedes. There is no reason why it should, and every reason to respect its essential character as a glimpse of the author's inmost feelings about his work, rather than an integral part of the work itself.

Vorspiel auf dem Theater

This 'Prelude' resembles *Zueignung* in being outside *Faust I* proper, not merely in terms of typographical layout, but also in the sense that it is saying something about the play from a standpoint external to it. But that standpoint is here a much less intimate one. A poet appears and speaks about his attitude to artistic creation, but he speaks as one figure alongside two others in this mini-drama, not with the solitary voice of lyrical self-expression we heard in the poem. It would be quite wrong to see Goethe himself simply in the Dichter and to identify the two other participants, the Direktor[16] and the Lustige Person, as opponents of genuine artistic aspirations. On the contrary, these three figures express different aspects of artistic achievement in general and theatrical achievement in particular, aspects which together characterise the play that is to come.

In essence, both the Direktor and the Lustige Person remind the poet that a dramatist has a special kind of artistic vocation that does not allow the luxury of creative aloofness. Drama fully succeeds only when artistic expression meets with public response in a performance which does justice to the text and strikes home to the audience. That is the ideal to which the three

[16] For simplicity's sake, the term 'Direktor' is used in this discussion; but this should not be taken to mean director in any modern Stanislavskian or Brechtian sense. What Goethe has in mind is as much a theatre owner and manager as anything else.

characters are collectively aspiring, and which they hope the ensuing production will attain; but individually each of them hankers after a less exacting goal. The poet, in particular, would like to be freed of the burden of appealing to his contemporaries (59-74). Yet his praise of 'Des Menschen Kraft, im Dichter offenbart' (157) centres on the power of art to 'move the hearts of all' (138), to take the apparent shapelessness of the given world and reveal its inner sense and coherence in a way that strikes a chord in everyone. This invites the response of the Lustige Person, 'So braucht sie denn, die schönen Kräfte' (158), and the Director's injunction, 'Gebt ihr euch einmal für Poeten, / So kommandiert die Poesie' (220-21). Art that claims to appeal to all cannot shirk exposure to general judgement, especially not dramatic art, which is fully realised only in performance.

The Direktor wants his theatre to be a financial success and knows very well that only the real public pays real money. No philistine, he respects the poet's aspirations and scruples, but encourages him to channel his talent into directions that will get him an audience. And the Lustige Person may be a clown by profession, but he is not a figure of fun here. He speaks up for the audience's legitimate wish, once it has paid its money, to be entertained as well as edified. Both are confident that the poet, protest as he may, can meet their requirements without sacrificing his artistic integrity; and there is a clear implication that his art will be all the better for it. What follows, we are invited to reflect, is an attempt to do justice to the demands of all three figures.

Prolog im Himmel

Like *Zueignung* and *Vorspiel auf dem Theater*, this scene stands before the title *Der Tragödie erster Teil* with which *Faust I* proper begins. It is a Prologue to the entire drama, not just that first part which Goethe was laying before the public in 1808 (and which may well have been all he was confident of ever actually completing at that time). But it cannot be left aside without forfeiting the key to the wager between Faust and Mephistopheles.

Goethe had access to the Faust material through two channels: the *Faustbuch*, and the puppet plays on the life of Faust frequently performed at fairs during his childhood.[17] These often began with a council of devils where the plan to ensnare Faust is hatched: since God has no hand in starting it, no problem about divine benevolence is raised. When Goethe substitutes an assembly in the courts of Heaven, especially one with clear allusions to the Book of Job, he emphasises from the start that divine goodness (or its secular analogue: the goodness of the world itself) is at question in Faust's destiny.[18]

Comparison with Goethe's biblical model for the heavenly council is revealing:

> The day came when the members of the court of heaven took their places in the presence of the LORD, and Satan was there among them. The LORD asked him where he had been. 'Ranging over the earth,' he said, 'from end to end.' Then the LORD asked Satan, 'Have you considered my servant Job? You will find no one like him on earth, a man of blameless and upright life, who fears God and sets his face against wrongdoing.' Satan answered the LORD, 'Has not Job good reason to be God-fearing? Have you not hedged him round on every side with your protection, him and his family and all his possessions? Whatever he does you have blessed, and his herds have increased beyond measure. But stretch out your hand and touch all that he has, and then he will curse you to your face.' Then the LORD said to Satan, 'So be it. All that he has is in your hands; only Job himself you must not touch.' And Satan left the LORD's presence.[19]

Satan in this biblical text is not the force of evil of post-Babylonian demonology, but a 'fault-finder'. Yahweh singles

[17] The very distant ancestor of these plays was Christopher Marlowe's *Dr Faustus*, but Goethe seems not to have read the English masterpiece until some years after *Faust I* was published.

[18] For a comprehensive survey of biblical references in *Faust I*, see *20*.

[19] Job 1, 6-12, New English Bible version.

out Job as someone who is blameless, but Satan is unimpressed. Job only serves Yahweh because he is well rewarded for doing so: take away the benefits and the devotion will go with them. Sure he can prove Satan wrong, Yahweh gives Satan power, first over Job's family and possessions, then (in a later passage) over 'his bone and his flesh'. The situation has some of the preconditions for a wager: disagreement between two parties about future events; and agreement about what would settle the dispute. In the Bible Goethe knew, there is even the *language* of a wager. Luther underlined Satan's confidence in Verse 11 with a colloquial expletive: 'aber recke deine Hand aus, und taste an alles, was er hat: *was gilt's*, er wird dir ins Angesicht absagen?'. Luther was not suggesting that Yahweh and Satan actually had a bet on about Job: in the speech of his day, 'was gilt's' — 'what's it worth (to you)' — was just a turn of phrase like the similar expression in 'I'll bet he'll be late'. But the allusion probably stirred Goethe's imagination.

The Book of Job may well also have suggested the opening motif of the *Prolog im Himmel*. In Job 38.7 the 'Gottessöhne' assembled before Yahweh are said to have witnessed creation and sung hymns of praise at the sight. When the curtain opens on the deliberately stagey Heaven of the 'Prolog', the angels are singing those praises still.

The archangels' song (243-70) looks at first sight like a paean to stability, and so it is. Yet on closer inspection it also reveals the collapse of a shared view of cosmic order. Dante used the Ptolemaic model of the universe — a set of concentric revolving crystal spheres with the earth stationary at the centre — because he thought it literally, as well as symbolically, true.[20] Milton used the same model consistently in *Paradise Lost* because it was for him an eloquent expression of spiritual truths about mankind's place in creation, though he knew it was physically false. But the song Goethe has given to the archangels yields no consistent physical picture. The universe described in Raphael's stanza is plainly geocentric: the sun, attached to its crystal sphere like its 'fraternal' companion heavenly bodies, is completing its 'prescribed' motion around the earth (243-46).

[20] See *10*.

However, in Gabriel's stanza, the rotation of the Earth on its own axis is held responsible, in Copernican fashion, for the alternation of day and night (251-54); and his closing lines (257-58) seem to say that the earth has orbital motion too. You could build a working model of Dante's universe, or of Milton's; but the system described in these stanzas, however poetically powerful, is mechanically unintelligible. It would be too fanciful to see here an anticipation of modern relativity, which dissolves any conflict between geocentric and heliocentric models by making both of them irrelevant; but the absence of a single coherent physical picture to serve as a metaphor for universal order (moral and spiritual, as well as physical) signals from the very start how unlike the worlds of Dante and Milton the universe of *Faust* really is. This is a world where perceived order is a matter of individual viewpoint, not of common vision.

Though geocentric, this universe is not centred on man. Indeed, human beings receive not a mention in the archangels' praises of creation. In this more subtle respect, the natural world they describe is very much that seen by the new science, which refused to understand the world as the outcome of divine provision for human needs. It held that man was related to the world, not because it was made specially for him (the medieval view) but because he was one part of the system of nature. His sole privilege within that system lay in the power to understand it, to grasp how nature worked according to its own laws. It is the poetry of such self-sufficient ordered diversity that the archangels extol.

And poetry, like virtually everything else in *Faust I*, is what these opening verses are.[21] The metre of the archangels' song is striking, but not common within the play: we shall not hear it

[21] It is hard to do justice in analytical prose to the range and power of this play's poetic language. Unless it is read with ears attuned to music, rhyme and rhythm, one of its principal modes of conveying meaning is overlooked. Yet it would be tedious to scrutinise poetic effects everywhere they occur, especially if that involved expounding the rudiments of scansion. I have adopted the rather unsatisfactory remedy of examining only a few salient instances where poetic effects convey substantial meaning, in the hope that readers will be encouraged to apply similar techniques more widely in their study of the text; and to keep the necessary nuts and bolts of German prosody accessible without being too obtrusive, I have assembled them in an appendix, which anyone puzzled by the terminology used to describe the verse should consult as needed.

often again, but when we do, its recurrence will be significant.
The four-foot iambic metre with *Kreuzreim*, alternate feminine
rhymes giving an additional unstressed syllable to every other
line, is maintained with a regularity which is striking in view of
the German language's natural resistance to such a rhythmic
pattern:

> Die Sonne tönt nach alter Weise
> In Brüdersphären Wettgesang,
> Und ihre vorgeschriebne Reise
> Vollendet sie mit Donnergang. (243-46)

The one deviation from this pattern is all the more impressive:

> Und schnell und unbegreiflich schnelle
> Dreht sich umher der Erde Pracht; (251-52)

where the inverted stress on 'dreht' seems to give the earth an
extra tweak of spin; and the impression of continuous pulses of
energy sustaining the movement is extended by the 'r' sounds, of
two different qualities, in each of the line's stressed syllables.

Energy securely contained within serene order is the
rhythmical import of all these lines, upon which their content
builds. Raphael begins the chorus with wonder at a sun that is
completing its orbit attached, like the moon and planets, to its
crystal sphere, resonating at its own distinct pitch and so sharing
literally in the cosmic harmony. Gabriel sings of the earth,
revolving on its axis so that day succeeds night and the rocks
against which the sea beats are caught up, for all their com-
parative stability, in the ceaseless motion. Michael's verse moves
still closer in to the earth. What he sees there falls under the
eighteenth-century aesthetic category of the 'sublime', that is, of
things that inspire delight mingled with fear, rather than purely
pleasurable joy in human beholders. It is important that such
things are here very much a part of the Creator's praiseworthy
design, whereas there was a strong orthodox tradition that

ascribed 'sublimity' in nature to the Fall, which was said to have introduced violence and grandeur into nature in contrast to God's original plan for a mild and pastoral Eden as man's dwelling place.[22] Then Michael's gaze and song move swiftly away from the storm-tossed earth to the calm of the divine presence, with an ease that suggests these are not two fundamental contraries, but opposite poles within an overall stability.

All this harmony and beauty in creation is, however, perceived without reference to mankind: when the existence of human beings is first mentioned, it is by Mephistopheles, and as evidence of a grave imperfection which the archangels have somehow overlooked. Like his Hebraic ancestor, Mephistopheles enters the heavenly court as a fault-finder; but the object of his criticism is more comprehensive. Immediately he calls into question the archangels' glorification of the created world as dynamically harmonious perfection.

Mephistopheles's speech rhythms throw a spanner into the metrical works. His first four lines (271-74) retain the rhyme pattern of the archangels' song, but add an extra stress. At first, the regular alternation of stressed and unstressed syllables is carried over from the angelic chorus. But that alternation abruptly collapses, shaking us rudely out of regular metre, at the 'mich auch', where Mephistopheles refers to his own presence. Two adjacent stressed syllables are followed by no less than four unstressed ones — just about as much disruption as a metrical scheme can stand in German without collapsing entirely:

> Da du, o Herr, dich einmal wieder nahst
> Und fragst, wie alles sich bei uns befinde,
> Und du mich sonst gewöhlich gerne sahst,
> So siehst du mich auch unter dem Gesinde.
> (271-74)

From this point onwards, the scene is predominantly in madrigal verse, which will be the most common mode of expression for

22 See *5*, pp.97-117.

both Faust and Mephistolpheles, the two characters who partake least of divine perfection: Mephistopheles because he scorns it, Faust because he longs for it and is racked by its remoteness from him.

It is important to appreciate what is old and what new in the dialogue that now develops between Mephistopheles and Der Herr. As the passage from Job shows, a satanic figure hobnobbing with the Almighty is not just a piece of eighteenth-century irreverence. But whereas the Satan of the biblical narrative found fault with one man's righteousness, Mephistopheles finds fault with the very universe itself because mankind in general exists within it. What the archangels have sung about 'Sonn' und Welten' may be all very fine, he concedes with mock graciousness (279). But what about man? Can a universe that includes such a confused, tormented and restless kind of creature really be all that harmonious and perfect? The implication that the creation of man was God's great error, irreparably spoiling his handiwork, is plain when Mephistopheles mismatches the angelic '... Sind herrlich wie am ersten Tag' (270) with the deliberately clod-hopping '... Und ist so wunderlich als wie am ersten Tag' (282).

The notion that the gift of 'Vernunft', 'den Schein des Himmelslichts' as Mephistopheles calls it — no doubt relishing the pun on 'radiance' and '(delusory) appearance' —, both specifies man's nature and causes his problems (280-92), is ancient and familiar. Equally traditional is the suggestion that the possession of freedom, the mark of human dignity in the divine image, has made the human race out of place in an otherwise orderly cosmos: what should have raised man above other creatures has abased him below them. What sets this dialogue in a modern context, however, is the absence of any suggestion that this condition is the consequence of Original Sin. Mephistopheles and Der Herr both plainly accept that this tormented restlessness is bound up with the very nature of humanity: human beings are just as they were meant to be in the plan of creation, they have not brought their unfortunate conditions upon themselves by setting their wills against that plan. Where Mephistopheles and Der Herr significantly differ is in the

perspective from which they see these agreed matters. Here we
have the first introduction of the essential motif of development,
in close association from the start with that of the wager. Where
Mephistopheles believes that what now is will always be, Der
Herr founds his confidence on what is yet to emerge. And dis-
agreements about the future in a context of agreement about the
present often lead, as happens here, to a wager. The wager
centres on the destiny of Faust; but its import is, quite literally,
universal.

Just as the biblical Yahweh abruptly names Job as someone
proof against Satan's jaundiced view of the human capacity for
righteousness, so Der Herr suddenly moves from the general to
the specific with the question, 'Kennst du den Faust?' (299).
Mephistopheles seems puzzled at the thought that Faust, of all
people, should be somehow an exception to the general run of
humanity. Yet Der Herr claims Faust as his exemplary servant:
he sees Faust as he is now in the same way that a gardener views
a sapling fruit tree, valuing it because he foresees the fruit it may
one day bear, whereas Mephistopheles sees in Faust, in mankind
in general, and indeed in the entire creation, only an eternal and
intolerable sameness despite endless universal movement.

The wager that crystallises out of their disagreement
establishes the thematic framework of the play from its cosmic
perspective. What is at stake is the goodness of creation itself. If
Mephistopheles proves to be right about Faust, he is *a fortiori*
right about mankind in general. And if he is right about
mankind in general being a grave flaw in the harmony of
creation, he will have made good his claim that the existence of
human beings, with their unique powers of 'Vernunft', is a
cosmic error best remedied by annihilation. To fulfil his role as
spirit of negation, Mephistopheles badly needs to win this bet: so
badly that, as we shall see, he will take on another bet, with
Faust, fully intending to lose it so that the wager concluded in
Heaven can be won.

The wager's terms are couched chiefly in the metaphor of a
journey towards a distant goal. As Mephistopheles proposes it,
his speech shifts towards the 'angelic' metre, which Der Herr
sustains for his three lines of assent, confirming by the acoustic

reference that the truth of the archangel's picture of a compre-
hensively harmonious universe is at issue.

> MEPHISTOPHELES.
>
> [Was wettet Ihr? Den sollt Ihr noch verlieren!
>
> Wenn Ihr mir die Erlaubnis gebt,]
> Ihn meine Straße sacht zu führen!
>
> DER HERR.
> Solang er auf der Erde lebt,
> So lange sei dir's nicht verboten.
> Es irrt der Mensch, solang er strebt. (312-17)

Faust then is on a journey; and the question is which road that
journey will take him along. Where Satan was given powers of
spectacular violence against Job's property and person, bringing
him swiftly to an evident time of trial, Mephistopheles asks for
permission to lead Faust 'sacht' — gently, subtly, barely per-
ceptibly — in a diabolical direction. Der Herr grants his request
with an aphorism that reminds us of the representative status of
Faust: not just Faust, but 'Der Mensch' goes astray as long as he
is trying to get anywhere; but this does not unduly worry Der
Herr, for the reason he gives in lines 328-29, still within the same
metaphor:

> Ein guter Mensch in seinem dunklen Drange
> Ist sich des rechten Weges wohl bewußt.

Such a 'good person', as Der Herr believes Faust to be, will be
kept, for all his wanderings and waverings, in essentially the
right path by the 'obscure urging' within him, whatever subtle
seductions Mephistopheles may offer from without. In the end,
all will be well, so the inevitable deviations are of little account
in Der Herr's eyes. In formulating his challenge to
Mephistopheles, Der Herr combines the metaphor of the

journey with another, whose philosophical ancestry is readily identifiable:

> Zieh diesen Geist von seinem Urquell ab
> Und führ ihn, kannst du ihn erfassen,
> Auf deinem Wege mit herab; (324-26)

The image of a 'primal spring' belongs to the neo-Platonic notion that creation is an outflowing of the divine being.[23] The natural cycle of a watercourse is used to symbolise a cosmic cycle in which created beings, after a time of dispersal and estrangement from their divine source, are gathered together into original unity once more. The fusion of this metaphor with that of the journey adds a characteristically eighteenth-century element: the neo-Platonic cycle becomes an ascending spiral. Faust is not simply moving in a circular path eventually leading back to his point of origin: he is also on an upward journey, so that the final goal, if he keeps on the 'right path', will be 'higher' than his starting point. Unless, that is, Mephistopheles can mislead Faust on to his own, descending, path on which all aspirations towards the ending of estrangement among human beings, and between the human spirit and the natural world, have been abandoned.

The wager Mephistopheles proposes, and Der Herr tacitly accepts,[24] resembles the later wager between Mephistopheles and Faust: in both instances, it is easier to see what Mephistopheles must do to win than to identify conditions that would prove he had lost. If Faust ever espouses Mephistopheles's attitudes, Mephistopheles will have indisputably won his wager with Der Herr: while Faust still despises those attitudes, he (and Der Herr) will not have lost their wagers — yet. Both Der Herr and Faust bet on their general confidence in an open future. Whatever that future proves to hold in detail, they are certain that Mephistopheles will never be able to claim

[23] See *5*, pp.146-54, and *31*, passim.

[24] Some commentators (e.g. Kobligk, *30*, pp.37-38) think Der Herr would not wager because he knows he is right: they obviously move in circles where people are sporting enough never to bet on things they feel sure about.

victory; and for them the indefinite postponement of defeat is victory enough.

The scene closes with Der Herr and Mephistopheles taking turns at patronising each other. Der Herr says his piece first, then disappears to the clatter of stage machinery ('*Der Himmel schließt sich*' is not a stage direction that can be obeyed quietly in the eighteenth-century theatre).[25] He assures Mephistopheles that he really quite likes him, because he does such a useful job in spite of himself. His type of 'negating spirit' stops human beings sinking into lethargy (though that particular vice did not figure in the earlier catalogue of what was wrong with mankind: rather the reverse). So from the heavenly perspective of the *Prolog*, Mephistopheles's activity appears not simply harmless but actually beneficial. But the play itself will offer another, very different, perspective upon all that Mephistopheles stands for; and that perspective, the viewpoint from which the drama comes into focus on an earthbound plane, will make Der Herr's breezy cheerfulness difficult for less exalted beings to share.

Mephistopheles has the *Prolog*'s last word, though Der Herr has not stayed to listen. The dismissal of his diabolical pretensions has obviously not upset him. He leaves us with a bit of banter about how he likes to keep on good terms with 'the Old Man'. He seems not to worry that Der Herr has such a low estimation of his powers of destruction, perhaps because he is confident that in individual human lives they will strike home devastatingly enough. That confidence will be amply vindicated in the play that follows.

*   *   *

Nacht

Faust first appears with a monologue, his most characteristic mode of utterance: even when ostensibly speaking to others, he is more often than not talking to himself. Time and again, he tells himself about his experience, assesses it, notes his own

[25] A good idea of the kind of clanking and rumbling involved can be gained from the arrival and departure of the Queen of the Night in Ingmar Bergman's film of *The Magic Flute*.

responses to it as it happens, revealing the burden of self-consciousness laid upon mankind through the problematic gift of 'Vernunft'. To see Faust's difficulties as the consequence of too much thinking and too little living (as does, for example, Gillies, *24*, p.20) is to trivialise the issue: he embodies the absolute impossibility for a creature with reflexive awareness of living without thought.

Faust's first speech begins in *Knittelvers*.[26] Its characteristic bumpiness, when allied to his fierce discontent, gives physical expression to a spirit chafing against its bonds. But *Knittelvers* has too little expressive range to be sustained for long. At line 377, as Faust explains his resort to magic, the rhythm begins to modulate towards a more regular stress pattern (conjunctions of stressed syllables and strings of more than two unstressed syllables are avoided), and at line 386 it settles into four beat iambic lines, though with frequent stress inversions. The predominantly masculine rhymes and firmly end-stopped lines, however, preserve the sense of constriction, very different from the smooth flow which the 'angelic' metre achieves.

The scene begins and ends in Faust's 'confined room'. In the interim come two grand projects for flight, and two powerful visitations from outside. But despite all the expenditure of spiritual energy, there is no linear movement. As far as this scene goes, Mephistopheles's claim that Faust's insatiability gets him nowhere seems borne out.

In Faust's despairing comments on his learning and teaching, we see a characteristic combination of arrogance and humility. He despises scholars like Wagner, not for being ignorant, but for being blind to the worthlessness of what they can learn. He pretends to no more *substantial* knowledge than those he despises, only to a superior, and highly uncomfortable, insight into the vacuity of everything that passes for knowledge.

Faust now gives his first formulation of the kind of knowledge that would meet his aspirations, and which he hopes magic may provide:

---

[26] There is a fine analysis of the language of this speech in *6*, pp.22-25.

> Daß ich erkenne, was die Welt
> Im Innersten zusammenhält,
> Schau alle Wirkenskraft und Samen,
> Und tu nicht mehr in Worten kramen. (382-85)

Three things stand out here. First, Faust craves extensive and all-inclusive knowledge (direct 'Erkenntnis', not just abstract 'Wissen') of the sum total of objects and experiences which make up 'die Welt'. Secondly, extensiveness and variety alone are not enough: he wants to apprehend a single principle of coherence that binds all these manifold things and experiences together. And thirdly, he is convinced that coherence-in-variety is a central and fundamental feature of creation. Whatever principle it is that makes the world cohere, it is located at the world's very heart, 'im Innersten'.

Here we see something that escapes Mephistopheles. Faust's aspirations are as much an expression of faith as a sign of discontent: faith that the universe is indeed characterised by a combination of variety and coherence, so that a true vision of the world would bring an intense and simultaneous grasp of multiplicity and unity. The source of Faust's anguish is that, though this vision can be specified, it seems beyond human experience, so that faith never gives way to knowledge. But the anguish testifies to Faust's abiding conviction that the goal is real and desirable, however unattainable it may seem. The sturdiness of this conviction is analogous to Job's faith in the inscrutable righteousness of Yahweh; it is what makes Faust the faithful 'servant' of a creator whose divinity is felt in the dynamic stability and manifold unity of the world.

The moonlight breaking through his murky window pane inspires a new view of his predicament. He is cut off from the state of union with nature into which mankind was first created, and the pursuit of knowledge, meant to overcome that division, has actually widened it:

> Statt der lebendigen Natur,
> Da Gott die Menschen schuf hinein,
> Umgibt in Rauch und Moder nur
> Dich Tiergeripp' und Totenbein. (414-17)

The living integration of man into nature has been replaced by a
fallen state in which the human mind 'murders to dissect', vainly
seeking the living truth in the dessicated skeletons of long-dead
creatures. (The motif recurs at lines 668-75, where Faust speaks
of his scientific apparatus as instruments designed to torture
nature, a notion Goethe used in his own anti-Newtonian
polemic.) The remedy that occurs to him is to flee his confined
study and seek the wide spaces of nature (418). But he is not
planning to keep a goat and grow his own vegetables: he pictures
himself wandering through the landscape, book in hand; a book
of occult lore, to be sure, but still a reminder that he is seeking
experience of nature, not as a set of objects, but as a body of
symbols requiring interpretation. If nature's signs can be
unlocked, he will achieve communion with spiritual entities
behind external forms, and a knowledge of the inmost workings
of the world — the culmination, not the abandonment of his
intellectual quest:

> Und wenn Natur dich unterweist,
> Dann geht die Seelenkraft dir auf,
> Wie spricht ein Geist zum andern Geist. (423-25)

That it is such knowledge which matters to him, rather than the
Great Outdoors where he first pictured himself receiving it, is
emphasised when Faust, opening the book before leaving his
study, is so captivated by what he finds that the projected flight
is abandoned.

His reaction to the symbol of the macrocosm shows a psychological pattern with which the play will make us extremely
familiar. Initial elation, followed by reflection on that elation,
passing into disillusionment and thoughts on what that disillusionment implies. As his gaze falls upon the symbol, Faust's
speech shifts into the madrigal verse which is to be so characteristic of both him and Mephistopheles. Unlike the 'trocknes
Sinnen' (426) which separated him from the objects of his
studies, the sight of the macrocosm seems to invigorate and
rejuvenate Faust by catching him up into the dynamism which it
symbolises. This is a representation of the universe, not as a

'dry' mechanism, but as a vast living being in which each of the myriad parts sustains and shares in a life greater than its own. Here nature is shown forth as various yet unified, complex yet organised, dynamic yet stable: the macrocosm, in other words, is a figure for precisely that knowledge which Faust seeks. But it does not itself convey the experience of universal unity-in-variety which it represents; and indeed, the fact that a symbolic representation of that unity-in-variety is needed before human minds can grasp it serves to increase Faust's awareness of the gulf between himself and the experience he craves, which the symbol had at first seemed to bridge. Hence the abrupt change of mood pivoting on two senses the same word: 'Welch Schauspiel! Aber ach! ein Schauspiel nur!' (454). A splendid spectacle to behold; but also something which stands in the same relationship to what it signifies as a play — the other sense of Schauspiel — does to real life. It is not the real thing, and nothing less than a direct apprehension of what the sign of the macrocosm indirectly portrays will do for Faust. Accordingly Faust turns the page with an ill-tempered feeling that he has been cheated.

What he now finds is a very different kind of sign. The macrocosm was a symbolic representation of the universe, not a being in its own right. But the Erdgeist is a spiritual being, over whom the sign in the book promises power. When the spirit appears, it identifies itself as the creative energy that weaves the fabric of the visible world, giving life and dealing death to the countless passing forms which are created and destroyed in nature's inexhaustible dynamism (501-509).[27] Though Faust feels exhilarated and intoxicated by the sign, and filled with courage to take all the world's joys and woes upon himself, that courage is soon to be sorely tried. Even before it is summoned, the Erdgeist makes its proximity felt in a sinister fashion: Faust's speech moves into broken bursts of free verse as the power of the spirit begins to overwhelm him; and when it obeys his call he finds to his dismay that he cannot look upon it. Far from being subservient to the magician who has compelled its presence, the Erdgeist scorns his presumption, his inability even to look at the

---

[27] For a perceptive, though diffusely argued, discussion of the destructive and threatening component in the Erdgeist, see *34*, pp.148-64.

spirit whom he felt was 'closer' to him than the remote spectacle of the macrocosm. It stays only to mock his weakness before leaving unbidden with a devastating reply to Faust's desperately repeated claim of close relationship: 'Du gleichst dem Geist, den du begreifst, / Nicht mir' (512-13).

These parting words strike home to Faust because they suggest that even in this direct encounter there is a falsifying barrier between his perceiving self and realities outside him. Faust, the spirit says, resembles his conception of the Erdgeist, not the spirit itself.[28] The shattering force of this rebuke is still present in the next phase of Faust's solitary meditations, when he condemns existence in a physical body as a barrier between the human soul and true experience. But before he develops such thoughts he is interrupted by Wagner.

Like the peasants who toast Faust in *Vor dem Tor* and the young student who seeks his advice in *Studierzimmer II*, Wagner serves to show us that Faust's low estimation of his own scholarship and wisdom is not shared by those around him. But we can also see why Faust is angered, rather than heartened, by a veneration inspired by things he holds worthless. Faust has just been engaged in an anguished encounter with the spirit of nature's boundless dynamism: Wagner assumes he was practising verse declamation and is anxious to pick up a few tips. Faust responds to Wagner's interest in rhetoric (aptly defined as 'the art of making people interested in what they know already'[29]) by advocating the artless expression of intense personal feeling (530-57). And he counters Wagner's enthusiasm for the scholarly reconstruction of the past with his newly awakened sense of the barriers consciousness erects between the seeker after knowledge and the objects of knowledge:

---

[28] I can see no other sensible reference for 'dem Geist, den du begreifst'. If it referred to Faust's own spirit, it would be a tautology; and if it referred to Mephistopheles, which Mason (*34*, p.164), for example, claims is the only reasonable supposition, it would be both false and incomprehensible to Faust, who has yet to meet Mephistopheles. Truisms or lies are hardly the Erdgeist's *métier*.

[29] By Dr P. Brady, Birkbeck College, in an unpublished paper.

Was ihr den Geist der Zeiten heißt,
Das ist im Grund der Herren eigner Geist,
In dem die Zeiten sich bespiegeln (577-79)

As Faust reflects after showing Wagner the door, the contrast between the two exchanges he has just engaged in could not be greater (606-607). In the first, which he solicited, he was rudely rebuffed: in the second, which was forced upon him by an eager would-be disciple, he found only 'schales Zeug' (603). But at least Wagner, by reminding him of how his aspirations set him apart from the people around him, has compensated for the sense of utter dejection in which the Erdgeist left him (608-613). He can now reflect with more self-possession upon the Erdgeist's brief apparition; and the result is despair of ever finding what he seeks while confined within a physical body. His recourse to magic, like his project to explore nature with occult lore as his guide, implied that the conventional path to knowledge is a false trail which can be abandoned in favour of a better one. That belief has now vanished. The accretion of burdensome 'fremder Stoff', he now believes, inevitably blocks any spiritual quest by a being of flesh and blood (634-39); and human actions themselves, not just external resistances, actually impede the advances they are meant to further (632-33). The entire contents of his room, the books and apparatus he has acquired and inherited, now seem mountainous evidence for this view; until, spotting among them a phial of poison, he undergoes another abrupt change of mood and plan: he resolves to kill himself in order to liberate his spiritual nature from its physical confinement. Instead of a violent current hemmed in by its banks, his spirit will become calm and boundless like the ocean (698-701); or, he will be swept away from an earthbound existence in a fiery chariot which will take him to 'Sphären reiner Tätigkeit' (705) where the writ that puts barriers between aspiration and activity does not run. He hesitates only through a doubt about whether a creature so recently abject in the face of the Erdgeist deserves such glorious liberation; but he overcomes this scruple by reminding himself of the courage which suicide requires. Unlike Hamlet, who fears the 'dreams' which the 'sleep' of death may bring, Faust's terror is that death may bring mere annihilation, the absolute negation of that fuller being which is the whole motive of his act (719). Since he is running the most terrible risk anyone with a hunger for a fuller existence can imagine, he judges himself worthy of the reward he will gain if his fear proves groundless.

In the remainder of this scene, Faust is affected by two reminiscences of his youth. The first is brought by the engraved crystal bowl from which he proposes to drink the poison. He recalls convivial evenings when this bowl made the rounds, part of the ritual of happy fellowship; but these memories of shared joys have no power over him. Very different is the effect of the Easter singing which invades his study. Again, we see an instant reaction which Faust's conscious mind then tries to catch up with. He feels the bowl 'violently' pulled from his lips as he is on the point of drinking: only afterwards does he first identify the sound which has so swiftly caused yet another change of course, then understand how and why it has had such an effect. The Easter message as such means nothing to him; but it does recall his youthful feelings at Eastertide, feelings which were full of promise for an earthly future in which his imagination could feel at home in a world of its own making and yet also of this earth, a world where human creativity and natural regeneration seemed capable of working together. Faust has been reminded that his aspirations are bound up with earthly experience, that he wishes to extend and transcend the bounds of that experience, not depart from it altogether. Nothing has been solved; but Faust has clarified that he belongs to the earth, and that it is on earth, in earthly life, that his quest must take place.

Vor dem Tor

For nearly a hundred lines (808-902) the 'Spaziergänger aller Art' hold the stage. In a pageant of energy, sound and colour, the human richness of the world Faust had been on the point of abandoning passes before us. When Faust does appear, paying tribute to the inhabited earth which has regained him, his words are unlike anything else we ever hear from him (903-940). For once he refers to people collectively ('they') without pity, condescension or contempt. And he expresses, uniquely, a sensation of joy shared with all those around him. The metrical skeleton of Faust's first speech is the 'popular' *Knittelvers*; but it has a strong injection of the regular dactylic rhythms commonly associated with levity and excitement. Winter, grown senile, has withdrawn to the hills, able only to send the odd hail shower against the advancing greenery of the new season. 'Bildung und Streben', emerging new forms in their energetic growth, are everywhere. The flowers have yet to arrive, but in their stead the countryside is decked out with people in their spring clothes. From line 915 on, Faust's speech lays out a panoramic landscape and populates it with figures: people thronging out of the town gate, wandering through orchards and fields, sailing across and along the river, visible in their festive colours even on the distant mountain slopes, while the sounds of village merrymaking are carried on the breeze. Here, for a time, everyone feels part of a common enjoyment of nature: and that feeling gives them a joyful sense of their own humanity, so that people of all ages and stations (the double reference of 'groß und klein' (939)) seem to call out triumphantly: 'Hier bin ich Mensch, hier darf ich's sein.' (940).[30]

Wagner's pernickety disdain for what so delights Faust ('I'm only here for the intellectual conversation') throws into relief Faust's appetite for robust pleasures, which will surface again during the Walpurgisnacht.[31] But there is nothing sinister about

[30] We should not let Faust's habitual self-reference mislead us into thinking that this line is his unique response to what he describes: the whole force of the passage lies in the exceptional fact that, for once, his feelings are in tune with a collective emotion, and he is delighted that it is so. That is why the colon at the end of line 939, which marks out the exclamation 'Hier bin ich Mensch ...' as a kind of quotation of what each and everyone is saying, is so important. Punctuation in *Faust* is a matter of unending scholarly dispute. But all the editions I have been able to consult agree on this colon, with the striking exception of the *Hamburger Ausgabe*, which, until the eleventh edition (1981), had a full stop, isolating the exclamation as Faust's private sentiment. Bizarrely, the 1981 revision substitutes a semi-colon: like its predecessor, this deviation from the accepted text is undertaken without editorial comment.

[31] Many critics follow Wagner. Gillies (*24*, p.34) finds the image of popular merriment 'not a gratifying one', and Atkins (*6*, p.34), calling Faust's delight 'facile', can hardly wait for the drama to move back on to 'a higher plane'. 'Lord, what would they say ...'

the company Faust finds himself in here. The old peasant proposes a toast in stark contrast to the words with which Faust had earlier prepared to down the poison draught: may Faust live for as many years as the goblet contains drops of wine (989-90), a wish that regards the prolongation of life as supremely desirable. Faust calls it an 'Erquickungstrank' (991) in more than a literal sense: the feeling of well-being among his fellow human beings in the rejuvenated countryside is dispelling the despondency that befogged his study. But the clouds close in again the moment the old peasant thanks Faust for what he and his father did for the community during the plague. With a curt admonition to thank God, not him, Faust passes on.

The well-meant gratitude has destroyed Faust's joy in the inhabited landscape (1022-1055). Now he recalls looking back on the town from this spot and praying desperately for an end to the plague which his father's remedies were powerless to cure. In these 'hills and valleys' (1051) now filled with colourful life, Faust and his father with their dubious potions killed off more people than the disease they were supposed to be fighting. And it is a measure of his integrity that he is devastated to be praised for his misdeeds (1030, 1054-55).

Unable to see why Faust is upset, Wagner can offer him no consolation. Yet so powerful and unaccustomed was his earlier sense of shared elation that Faust himself tries to re-create it: 'Doch laß uns dieser Stunde schönes Gut / Durch solchen Trübsinn nicht verkümmern!' (1068-69), remarkable words indeed from someone who normally makes little effort to look on the bright side. He evokes the evening landscape (time passes quickly on this symbolic day) in what seems at first a companion piece to his opening speech. But now the metre is *Madrigalvers*, and the overall movement is much more typical of Faust: from the lyrical description of the natural scene, he passes into an intense longing for something characteristically unattainable. The sun is departing, Faust reflects, in order to spread life in other parts of the globe; and he longs for wings that would allow him to fly eternally in the sun's wake, seeing always the daylight ahead of him and darkness behind. The immediate experience becomes simply a source of imagery to conjure up a less concrete desire: the longing to make the ephemeral a permanent possession. This is not, of course, a wish that technology can fulfil; it is at bottom a metaphysical craving to experience beauty and yet escape the transience which is its precondition. Such has been the power of this day of general reawakening over Faust, with its combined impressions of resurgent natural vitality and 'volkstümlich' *joie de vivre*, that even this more esoteric longing figures as something he shares with mankind, not as a higher aspiration that sets him apart:

> Doch ist jedem eingeboren,
> Daß sein Gefühl hinauf und vorwärts dringt,
> Wenn über uns, im blauen Raum verloren,
> Ihr schmetternd Lied die Lerche singt (1092-95)

Just as in his first speech in this scene Faust shared the sense of well-being of 'groß und klein', so here the 'uns' makes his renewed sense of deprivation something he shares with everyone else: he does not here speak as the 'ich' of *Nacht*, tormented by a sense of solitary affliction, any more than his earlier delight was couched in the terms of solitary fulfilment we find in *Wald und Höhle*.[32]

To Wagner, such sentiments show Faust is having a 'grillenhafte Stunde': for his part, he prefers the pleasures of a venerable manuscript (1100-1109). Though Faust has had disparaging words enough to say about scholarship, he does not repeat them here, such is the extent of his new-found sentiment of general benevolence. Instead, he allows 'Geistesfreuden' their due, but tells Wagner to count himself lucky he knows of no other impulse. He, for his part, is torn in two by conflicting aspirations: on the one hand, towards immediate sensuous experience, on the other towards the heights of intellectual and spiritual achievement.

---

[32] Requadt (*37*, pp.101-02) draws on Goethe's *Farbenlehre* to show how the colour imagery in this passage underpins the impression of 'gleichgewichtige Einheit'.

Zwei Seelen wohnen, ach! in meiner Brust,
Die eine will sich von der andern trennen:
Die eine hält in derber Liebeslust
Sich an die Welt mit klammernden Organen;
Die andre hebt gewaltsam sich vom Dust
Zu den Gefilden hoher Ahnen. (1112-17)

These are probably the most often misunderstood and
inappropriately quoted lines in German literature. It cannot be
sufficiently emphasised that Faust is not in any sense speaking of
a moral conflict. The conflict is practical (though it has metaphysical roots and implications). Goethe is not Schiller; still less
is he the Wilhelminian caricature of Schiller, Nietzsche's 'Moral-
trompeter von Säckingen'. Faust does not say he would like to
pursue spiritual goals if only his sensual appetites were not in the
way (nor does he say the reverse). There is no relative evaluation
here of the 'zwei Seelen' and their desires. What Faust laments is
that the two souls cannot live one life in one body without
rending it asunder by pulling in different directions at once.
With emotional, though not rational logic, he moves from this
lament to a wish that some spirit of the air might carry him to
the land Baudelaire terms 'Anywhere out of the world', the
Shangri La of the romantic imagination in which the prosaic
categories of everyday life, which enforce such divisions, are
fused into something rich and strange. This *is* an escapist wish,
not a serious project (unlike some of the things Faust planned to
do in the earlier scene); yet it is ironically the uttering of
precisely this wish that shapes the rest of his life, for it brings
Mephistopheles to him. Wagner's warning against calling on
such spirits seems all of a piece with his general feebleness, so
that his remark that they 'Gehorchen gern, weil sie uns gern
betrügen' (1139), apposite as it will prove to be, is passed over by
Faust and audience alike. And his caution is purely theoretical.
Not Wagner but Faust sees and correctly interprets the sinister
motion of the poodle, circling about them and leaving a faint
trail of fire behind it: 'Mir scheint es, daß er magisch leise
Schlingen / Zu künft'gem Band um unsre Füße zieht' (1158-59).
In this, his first comment on Mephistopheles's conduct, Faust

correctly foresees that the 'future bond' between them will be in truth an ensnarement, an insight he never recovers until it is too late. But Wagner's prosaic eyes see nothing but 'Hundebrauch' in the dog's behaviour, and Faust's curiosity and apprehension are, for the time being, quelled.

Studierzimmer I

Faust returns to his study in the aftermath of an unusually happy day. His sense of well-being is expressed, in striking contrast to his normal speech patterns, in the 'angelic' metre. And in that metre he expresses a sense of primal unity felt as universal love among mankind and between man and God. He still noticeably uses the 'uns' (1181) which signifies a consciousness of common experience, taken up by 'unserm' in line 1196 and 'man' in line 1200. The notion of love harmoniously and closely binding all things together is underpinned by the chiasma in lines 1184-85:

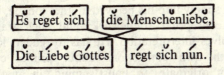

As in Heaven, the 'angelic' rhythm of universal harmony is interrupted by Mephistophelean objections, as the poodle's restlessness is reflected in Faust's abrupt move into madrigal verse at line 1186. He tries to bring the poodle into his own tranquil mood, modulating first into a reminiscence of the *Knittelvers* with prominent dactylic patterns which expressed joy at communal merriment in *Vor dem Tor*:

Wie du draußen auf dem bergigen Wege
Durch Rennen und Springen ergetzt uns hast,

then into the 'angelic' metre proper before continuing his reflections:

So nimm nun auch von mir die Pflege

ᵕ ́ ᵕ ́ ᵕ ́ᵕ ́
Als ein willkommner stiller Gast. (1190-93)

After the day's refreshment, the 'enge Zelle' is now cosy
rather than constricting, the lamp a welcoming refuge from the
gathering darkness outside; and in this atmosphere, an inner
light is kindled which inspires a mellow yearning ('Sehnen', not
the strenuousness of 'Streben') towards both the 'streams' of life
and its 'wellspring' (1200-1201). Once again, this is the neo-
Platonic image of the creative cycle as an outflowing of being,
expressing the same sentiment as lines 1184-85: the 'streams' of
life are the created universe, to which Faust now feels bound in
'Menschenliebe', and the yearning for the 'wellspring' is the love
of God.

But the poodle's growling destroys Faust's sense of inner
riches in harmony with an ample world. Since the 'inner flow'
has 'dried up' (1212) he seeks to nourish it from an external
source: divine revelation. For Faust the modern intellectual,
revelation cannot be humbly and passively received: he must
translate it, not simply into his beloved mother tongue, but also
into his own conceptual framework; and such translation
necessarily involves interpretation. He has to render 'logos' in
accordance with own convictions about primal creation.
Creation cannot originate, to Faust's mind, in anything so
derivative as a word: prior to the word is its meaning or
intention ('Sinn'). But creation is the supreme example of
effective action, and action depends not simply upon the agent's
intention, but upon his power ('Kraft'). Even this is not
primitive enough; and Faust is not satisfied that he has the right
word for the origin of all things until he writes 'Im Anfang war
die *Tat*' (1237).

For the twentieth-century reader, the force of this line is
buried under a tedious mound of mostly ribald quotation. Not
so for Goethe's contemporaries, who would have thought above
all of Fichte's notion of a primal deed in which cosmic subject
and cosmic object, having generated division through the mere
fact of coming into being, co-existed for an unrecoverable
moment in unity before falling into that divided condition from
which individuated selves must seek redemption through what

Fichte calls 'unendliches Streben'.[33] In the beginning, then, according to Faust's 'inspired' translation, was a dynamic unity pregnant with division, a paradise whose very nature produced a Fall into strife and discord from which the only escape lies in the re-attainment of the unity of subject and object on a higher level. Once the allusion is recognised, this notion of creation implies the particular path of salvation which Faust in his 'dunklem Drange' is trying to follow: which is why its utterance drives Mephistopheles into a frenzy of howling and barking, swiftly followed by a shedding of his canine disguise.

Apart from granting the Direktor's wish for spectacular stage effects, Mephistopheles's metamorphoses into the likenesses of ferocious beasts[34] brings him on to the scene with an aura of violent menace which we (and Faust) forget at our peril. It will never again be so apparent that Mephistopheles, despite his 'modern' bearing, has something of the fearsome powers and destructive designs of the traditional devil. Faust laughs when 'des Pudels Kern' turns out to be Mephistopheles as a 'fahrender Skolast' who wonders what all the fuss is about. He thinks it funny that such formidable apparitions should be 'really' no more than disguises for such an obviously harmless fellow. The less amusing thought, that precisely this harmless demeanour may be a cunning disguise, escapes him.

As Requadt observes (*37*, p.121), Mephistopheles's emergence in human shape gives Faust for the first time a partner with whom he can engage in cut-and-thrust dialogue. Introducing himself, Mephistopheles deploys at once his chief technique of deception, which is breathtakingly simple: he tells the truth. But he contrives to divert attention from the real import of what he

[33] An adequate account of what these terms mean in Fichte's philosophy would be too lengthy, and run the risk of suggesting that Goethe's play is somehow an embodiment of Fichte's ideas in particular. This is not the case. Faust's predicament and destiny in *Faust I* are indeed understood along lines suggested by German Idealist re-interpretations of the Fall; and Fichte may well have provided the term 'Streben' as well as the germ of the lines in question. But the intellectual framework of the play no more derives specifically from Fichte than it does from Kant or Schiller or Herder.

[34] The hippopotamus was not thought a cuddly creature in the eighteenth century. Thanks to Flanders and Swan (and Walt Disney) we simply cannot read lines 1254-55 as Goethe wrote them. Nor do similar influences let us respond to the comparison with an elephant (1311) quite as we are meant to.

is saying, so that the truth uttered is not properly heard. Deceptive truth is immediately visible in Mephistopheles's first self-definition as 'ein Teil von jener Kraft, / Die stets das Böse will und stets das Gute schafft' (1335-36). The *Prolog im Himmel* established that this is indeed Mephistopheles's role in the scheme of things; but this truth deceives because it suggests that the long-term creation of good painlessly cancels the evil intentions (and their realisation). The drama will show that that is far from the case. Mephistopheles continues with a frank and precise statement of how he is the adversary of Der Herr and of all that makes Faust Der Herr's faithful servant:

> Ich bin der Geist, der stets verneint,
> Und das mit Recht, denn alles, was entsteht,
> Ist wert, daß es zugrunde geht;
> Drum besser wär's, daß nichts entstünde (1338-41)

This is indeed the credo of evil from the play's cosmic perspective, the negation of Faust's faith in the essential goodness of creation and of his aspirations towards a direct apprehension of the goodness in its unity and variety, its dynamism and stability. All that comes into being in nature's endless creativity, Mephistopheles is saying, is utterly worthless: hence the best thing would be for nothing to come into being at all (with the metaphysical undertone of nothingness replacing being). Words such as these are what Faust must be made to utter if Mephistopheles is to win his wager with Der Herr.

The strategy of deception through truth-telling is sustained when Mephistopheles, oddly it might seem for someone who is supposedly crying his wares, laments the futility of his activities. He offers no untrue facts: only the carefully cultivated impression of ineffectualness is misleading. He cites the repeated failure of the powers of nothingness he represents: first their defeats in the battle of darkness against light (1346-58), then the repelling of all their onslaughts on the fabric of being (1362-1378). These lines emphasise that Mephistopheles sees growth and destruction as eternally opposed principles, not perceiving the 'Kette / Der tiefsten Wirkung rings umher' (261-62) which from the angels' perspective binds them into the same process. But the limitations of Faust's awareness emerge, too: taken in by Mephistopheles's self-deprecation (1359-61), he is unperturbed by his strangely cheerful willingness to consider trying 'something different' (1383-84). Mephistopheles is indeed already doing just that, though Faust has no idea of what this 'something different' is, and how intimately it involves him.

In Mephistopheles's departure, as in his arrival, seeming subservience masks a demonstration of power. Mephistopheles's claim to be trapped by the imperfectly drawn pentagram (1393-95) suggests he is subject to control. But that is precisely why Mephistopheles draws Faust's attention to his apparent inability to leave. It gives Faust a taste of power and makes him entertain the idea of a pact that would formalise such power over demonic forces and turn it to his benefit (1413-15). No sooner has Faust risen to the bait than Mephistopheles proves where the real power lies. He has no difficulty lulling Faust into a deluded dream and taking his leave without permission: 'Du bist noch nicht der Mann, den Teufel festzuhalten!' (1509) says Mephistopheles in his true scornful voice to the oblivious Faust to whose waking eyes he appeared subservient and ineffectual.

Studierzimmer II

To grasp the import of this scene we must see how Mephistopheles is continuing the cat-and-mouse game which he avowedly so enjoys (322). Mephistopheles's opening gambit, perhaps intended to counter the effect of his victory in the battle of wills over his departure, is to draw attention once more to the ritual rules governing the spirits: Faust, he points out, must invite him three times before he can cross the threshold (1531). Then, by studiedly banal interjections to the effect that 'things aren't as bad as all that, surely?' he goads Faust into two denunciations of his life. The first (1544-1571) is similar to much of what he had to say in *Nacht*; but the second (1583-1606), a superb crescendo of all-encompassing imprecation, attains an intensity of despair beyond anything Faust has so far expressed. Still, this passage, finely analysed by Requadt (*37*, pp.137-141), does not show 'agreement with [Mephistopheles's] point of view' (*24*, p.47). Faust is still remote from the cold cynicism of Mephistopheles's condemnation of existence. Far from revealing a belief that 'alles, was entsteht, ist wert, daß es zugrunde geht' the curses Faust hurls in the world's teeth express his furious conviction that a real and possible fuller existence is being withheld from him. Instead of denouncing all conceivable existence as worthless, he curses a creation which refuses him access to its treasures, and castigates everything that might make such deprivation seem tolerable.

A chorus of spirits intervenes, lamenting that Faust's curses have somehow accomplished what aeons of attack by Mephistopheles and his kin have failed to do: the 'beautiful world' has been shattered into fragments now bound for nothingness (1607-16). They enjoin Faust to build a new, more splendid world 'within his breast' and embark upon a new course of life in it (1617-26). It is hard to see what this exhortation means, and harder still to perceive what part the chorus's intervention plays in the scene, especially as it is far from clear just who these singing spirits are and where they stand in the spectrum between the angels and Mephistopheles.

In any case, Mephistopheles affects not to take Faust's bitter curses as seriously as the chorus of spirits does. He insinuates that Faust has no right to condemn life until he has seen more of it, and he offers his services as a guide to everything in worldly experience that Faust has missed through living in solitude 'Wo Sinnen und Säfte stocken' (1633). Faust asks 'Was soll ich dagegen dir erfüllen?' (1649), which is nearly the right question, but not quite. The price to be paid is indeed the most important thing to know; but by asking only what he personally will have to pay, Faust fails to imagine the full scope of the evil which Mephistopheles will unleash. Mephistopheles can say that all the devil demands is something by which Faust sets little store: control of his destiny in the hereafter. 'Das Drüben kann mich wenig kümmern' (1660), says Faust off-handedly, inviting Mephistopheles's obvious reply that, in that case, he has nothing to lose (1671).

Thus ill-advisedly reassured about the cost, Faust is still

sceptical about the goods on offer. Someone like
Mephistopheles, he remarks, could never even grasp what it is
Faust aspires to, let alone procure it (1675-77). He continues
with a catalogue of the kind of ephemeral trash which the devil
provides for the *Faustbuch* Faust, sarcastically pretending that
this is a list of the sort of things he desires (1678-87).
Mephistopheles affects to take the requests seriously.[35] He
would have to be quite uncharacteristically dim not to notice the
sarcasm; but he does not want to deflect the course of their conversation by acknowledging Faust's contempt at this point, so he
passes over it and makes a remark calculated to arouse Faust to
a new intensity of fastidious disdain: 'Doch, guter Freund, die
Zeit kommt auch heran, / Wo wir was Guts in Ruhe schmausen
mögen' (1690). The Mephistopheles who correctly characterised
Faust's elevated aspirations ('Nicht irdisch ist des Toren Trank
noch Speise' (301)) now makes a chummy offer of 'a quiet bit of
what you fancy' — to choose an approximately equivalent
English register — to his face. This must be monumental
stupidity or devilish cunning; and the context of the offer, as
well as the character who makes it, points clearly to the latter.

Formulating his ostensible conception of what Faust would
like in terms which he knows Faust will find contemptible,
Mephistopheles manoeuvres Faust into a deal. Faust remains
sure that he would not be satisfied by anything Mephistopheles
could give him; but he thinks he sees a way of harnessing
Mephistopheles's efforts to provide him with 'was Guts' to a
new project he has conceived, which shows the influence of
Mephistopheles's praise of worldly experience: 'Laß in den
Tiefen der Sinnlichkeit / Uns glühende Leidenschaften stillen!
(1750-51). And to make sure, as he thinks, that Mephistopheles
will do his best to provide him with whatever sensual experiences
can be procured, Faust defines what he would accept as a final
defeat for all he holds dear, and wagers that Mephistopheles will

[35] Some critics have been misled by Mephistopheles's reply into thinking these
are things Faust really wants. Buchwald (*14*, pp.64-65), who has obviously never
tried growing soft fruit, claims this is a list of impossible things, expressing the
absolute insatiability of Faust's cravings. Requadt (*37*, pp.152-55), taking the
same line, has to concede that many of the things Faust claims to want are all too
possible: his suggestion that Faust, carried away by enthusiasm, is simply picking
bad examples smacks of desperation rather than scholarly conviction.

never bring him to such a defeat.

Faust's first statement of what he would accept as damning defeat is a direct reaction to Mephistopheles's words about wanting a quiet bit of self-indulgence from time to time: 'Werd' ich beruhigt je mich auf ein Faulbett legen, / So sei es gleich um mich getan!' (1692-93). Faust will be lost in his own eyes if he can ever settle back to enjoy something without any sense of inadequacy or desire for something else. In his eagerness to get Mephistopheles to take up the wager, Faust stresses that he will still admit defeat even if the contented fulfilment is a momentary illusion wrought by guile:

> Kannst du mich schmeichelnd je belügen,
> Daß ich mir selbst gefallen mag,
> Kannst du mich mit Genuß betrügen:
> Das sei für mich der letzte Tag! (1694-97)

And Faust proposes an agreed sign that this 'deception' has been achieved:

> Werd' ich zum Augenblicke sagen:
> Verweile doch! du bist so schön!
> Dann magst du mich in Fesseln schlagen,
> Dann will ich gern zugrunde gehn! (1699-1702)

Faust, we should note, does not envisage himself ever uttering this phrase other than in a moment of delusion: he is setting Mephistopheles the difficult challenge of tricking him, not the impossible one of genuinely satisfying him. He thinks that by naming what seem attainable conditions for his own defeat he is goading Mephistopheles into believing the wager can be won. But Faust overestimates his own cleverness and underestimates Mephistopheles's duplicity. It never occurs to him that Mephistopheles might not *want* to win on the terms proposed, and that he is luring Faust into the wager in order to bring him to a different form of defeat than the one the wager envisages. Faust's failure to see this (which he shares with most critics) is ironic, because he himself takes on the wager, not in order to win, but because of the benefits he expects from his opponent's efforts to make him lose. The harder Mephistopheles tries, the more it will suit Faust. That is why Faust goes out of his way to emphasise how much effort he is going to expend to help his adversary win: 'Nur keine Furcht, daß ich dies Bündnis breche!' (1741) which is an assurance that he will enter body and soul into the experiences Mephistopheles will put in his way, thus, it would seem, making the disastrous delusion of momentary fulfilment easier to produce. But Faust has no fear of succumbing to such delusion: what he does have, as the essential motive of the wager from his side, is the hope that, by sheer accumulation through the aid of Mephistopheles's magic, he will attain something of that comprehensiveness and intensity of experience which he craves. Faust speaks of this new course as a lowering of his sights: 'In deinen Rang gehör ich nur, / Der große Geist hat mich verschmäht...' (1745-46); but he is still after a direct experience of unity in variety, an overcoming of the divisions that mark man's fallen state, this time through attempting to accumulate all the experience of mankind within a single self — a goal which he knows would destroy his individual selfhood if attained:

> Und was der ganzen Menschheit zugeteilt ist,
> Will ich in meinem innern Selbst genießen,
> Mit meinem Geist das Höchst' und Tiefste greifen,
> Ihr Wohl und Weh auf meinen Busen häufen,
> Und so mein eigen Selbst zu ihrem Selbst erweitern,
> Und, wie sie selbst, am End' auch ich zerscheitern.
>
> (1770-75)

This is obviously a project beyond the scope of natural human powers; only the assistance of Mephistopheles's magic makes its pursuit feasible, and Mephistopheles, so Faust believes, will be driven to lend that assistance in full measure by the prospect of winning the wager.

The fatal weakness of Faust's stratagem is the fact that Mephistopheles has no intention of trying to win. To bring this essential point home to us, Goethe uses the firm convention of

the eighteenth (and nineteenth) century European stage that
soliloquising characters utter their true thoughts. The conventional candour of monologue allows deceitful intentions
towards other characters, otherwise well concealed, to be laid
bare to the audience. We must set what Mephistopheles says to
Faust's face against what he says about his plans for Faust when
left for a moment alone with the audience:

> Den schlepp ich durch das wilde Leben,
> Durch flache Unbedeutenheit,
> Er soll mir zappeln, starren, kleben,
> Und seiner Unersättlichkeit
> Soll Speis' und Trank vor gier'gen Lippen
> [schweben;
> Er wird Erquickung sich umsonst erflehn,
> Und hätt' er sich auch nicht dem Teufel übergeben,
> Er müßte doch zugrunde gehn! (1860-67)

These lines are the key to understanding Mephistopheles's
strategy and tactics throughout the drama. To win the wager
with Faust, Mephistopheles would have to bring him to utter the
agreed formula of damnation. If only it could be done, that
would win Mephistopheles his wager with Der Herr as well, for a
contented Faust would no longer be Der Herr's faithful
'servant'. But unlike Faust, Mephistopheles has little appetite
for the impossible; and he is shrewd enough to know that
inducing Faust, even for a deluded moment, to feel unalloyed
well-being, is beyond his or anyone's powers. This speech
establishes that Mephistopheles is not going to make those
strenuous efforts to provide fulfilling experiences on which
Faust's hopes for the wager depend. Dragging someone through
a world of insipid trivialities, dangling food and drink before his
greedy lips but never letting him have the refreshment he pleads
for is hardly the way to make him beg a fleeting moment to
abide. The project Mephistopheles here reveals to the audience is
not to bring Faust towards a sense of fulfilment, but to lead him
through a series of frustrations until, no doubt, his disgust with
the world leads him to join in Mephistopheles's nihilistic con-

demnation of 'alles, was entsteht'.[36] That will never win him the wager with Faust. But Mephistopheles, intent above all on winning the wager made in heaven, plans to use the spurious wager with Faust as a means to that end. A Faust who found his tour of the world's weal and woe to be a forced march through a desert of banalities might finally lose all hope of anything better and join in the Mephistophelean condemnation of existence; and such a Faust would indeed have been, in the terms of Der Herr's challenge, 'drawn away from from his primal spring'. He would have lost his faith in the ultimate goodness of creation and the possibility of salvation through an apprehension of that goodness. And then Mephistopheles could indeed indulge in 'Triumph aus voller Brust', because Der Herr's confidence in Faust would have been proved false; and with Faust would fall Der Herr's defence of the perfection of a creation that encompasses man. The theodicy for which the *Prolog im Himmel* provides a framework would have failed.[37]

Faust consequently deludes himself when he thinks he has struck a cunning bargain: he is in fact Mephistopheles's dupe, the unwitting victim of a larger diabolical design. But that is not the only sense in which this scene shows us a Faust who is dangerously unaware of what his involvement with Mephistopheles is really about. We have passed over a passage which has too often been neglected. It concerns Mephistopheles's insistence on a written agreement: 'Nur eins — Um Lebens oder Sterbens willen / Bitt ich mir ein paar Zeilen aus' (1714) (a fine specimen of deceptive truth-telling, this, with

[36] In his analysis of this passage, Gillies (*24*, p.56), unlike most other critics, recognises Mephistopheles's 'expectation that Faust will renounce all his efforts in sheer disappointment and disgust'; but he does not explain how this expectation squares with the wager Mephistopheles has just made, nor does he hesitate, just two pages later, to resume the traditional assumption that Mephistopheles is trying to 'satisfy' Faust.

[37] On this cardinal point I disagree with the best of the younger generation of *Faust* scholars, Nicholas Boyle (*11*), who claims that *Faust I* can be understood in its own right without reference to the *Prolog im Himmel*, which is, he argues, not in a strict sense part of *Faust I* at all. But I simply cannot see how to make sense of Mephistopheles's words and conduct in *Studierzimmer II* (which, of course, belongs to the same phase of composition as the *Prolog im Himmel*) without bringing Mephistopheles's two wagers into consideration; and that gives *Prolog im Himmel* an extremely important part in the meaning of *Der Tragödie erster Teil*.

'a matter of life and death' deadened by a hackneyed phrase and
muffled under a casual introduction and a belittling reference to
'a line or two'). Mere pedantry, says Faust; but his gloss on this
judgement is just one of several ominous elements in these lines:
'Rast nicht die Welt in allen Strömen fort, / Und mich soll ein
Versprechen halten?' (1720). We shall find ourselves recalling
those words later, when it suits Faust to put greater faith in his
own promises. But there is more. Mephistopheles seems to share
Faust's scorn for this 'formality', saying that the precise format
does not matter, apart from one thing. The force of that one
thing, and the significance of Faust thinking it of no account, is
subtly suggested by the rhyme-pattern:

MEPHISTOPHELES. Wie magst du deine Rednerei	
Nur gleich so hitzig übertreiben,	a
Ist doch ein jedes Blättchen gut.	b
Du unterzeichnest dich mit einem Tröpfchen Blut.	b
FAUST. Wenn dies dir völlig Gnüge tut,	b
So mag es bei der Fratze bleiben.	a
MEPHISTOPHELES. Blut ist ein ganz besondrer Saft.	c
FAUST. Nur keine Furcht, daß ich dies Bündnis breche!	d
Das Streben meiner ganzen Kraft	c
Ist grade das, was ich verspreche.	d

(1734)

Though there is no traditional pact, and no fearsome document
to be recited, there is still a signature, and it is still in blood. For
the first, but certainly not the last time in the play, blood flows:
whenever it flows subsequently, it will always be in consequence
of the undertaking on which Faust is here embarking. Jocularity
masks menace, the old notions of dealings with the devil are
debunked, yet sinister elements of those notions still survive.
The single line in which Mephistopheles remarks on the 'quite
special' qualities of blood is something of an orphan, as far as
the movement of sense in the passage is concerned. One portion
of dialogue, with its own group of rhymes, seems to end just

before it, and, in the immediately following line, a new theme begins, as Faust passes over Mephistopheles's enigmatic remark and launches into his promise to try his hardest. But the rhyme of 'Saft' with 'Kraft' makes the link which Faust overlooks. The question of the cost is now being answered truly enough, though it was never properly asked: the engagement of all Faust's energies will, to Mephistopheles's delight, cause blood, though not Faust's own, to be shed.

The scene from which so much destruction will follow has a lighter coda in Mephistopheles's mildly satirical set-piece as student counsellor (1868-2049): then Faust returns, dressed for the journey, but worried that his long beard and all it stands for will prevent him being a debonair man of the world (2055-60). Mephistopheles assures him that a little self-confidence is all he needs: before long, though, he will be offering him something stronger from the witch's kitchen.

Auerbachs Keller

The first stop on Faust's course through the world shows him 'flache Unbedeutenheit' in plenty. It 'elaborates the Mephistophelean view of man' (*6*, p.62), and shows that Mephistopheles is carrying out the plan he confided to the audience, rather than trying to win his wager with Faust. Far from being 'merely vulgar' (*24*, p.58), the rumbustuous scene combines slapstick and spectacle, to strong theatrical effect, though it offers little for thematic analysis.

Hexenküche

Faust visits the witch's kitchen to be rejuvenated magically so that he can enter the world with the appetites and organs of a young man. Here he encounters a kind of magic very different from the one to which he first turned. The witch practises black magic: that is, she is in servitude to the forces of evil, and derives her powers from that servitude. The loathsome cauldron, the rowdy monkeys and general hocus-pocus are very different from the scholarly ambience of ritual magic, and Faust dislikes it all intensely. The way he says so emphasises how little he understands the realms he has entered. Scorning the 'Sudelköcherei' (2341) as ineffectual — but wrongly, for he is soon to find that, whatever else can be said about it, it works — he asks whether the rejuvenation cannot be carried out in a way he finds more congenial: 'Hat die Natur und hat ein edler Geist / Nicht irgendeinen Balsam ausgefunden?' (2345). Faust would prefer something that has itself been produced by nature, perhaps with the co-operation of some 'noble spirit' able to guide the working of natural principles without violating them. But he wants to undo what years of life and growth have made of him, and this cannot be done without such violation, symbolised by the grotesque place and its inhabitants.

As Mephistopheles is drawn into fun and games with the monkeys, Faust's eye is caught by the one item that seems different from the tawdry surroundings: the mirror in which he sees a recumbent (and presumably naked) figure who is the epitome of female beauty.[38] He at once begins to speak in a tone of intense delight, such as we have not heard since *Vor dem Tor*, very many lines ago:

> Was seh ich? Welch ein himmlisch Bild
> Zeigt sich in diesem Zauberspiegel!
> O Liebe, leihe mir den schnellsten deiner Flügel
> Und führe mich in ihr Gefild! (2429-32)

After the initial gasp of wonder, Faust's feelings expand into the two exclamations, the first running on into the next line, the second, starting in a line of extra length, rich in internal patternings of 'l' and 'f' sounds. Mephistopheles's blasé response (2441-43), implying that Faust's excitement is naive, has by contrast a flat alternation of stressed and unstressed syllables and no such richness of sound. Just as an image of the suffering to which he is oblivious lurks on the margin of the *Walpurgisnacht* revelries, so here the mirror is a window from the shoddy domain of magic on to natural beauty. But it is an

---

[38] The plain reference of Faust's 'ist das Weib so schön?' (2437) is generic woman. So speculation about the identity of the figure Faust sees is beside the point.

aspect of natural beauty of which Faust has remained too long ignorant; and he needs the aid of magic if that ignorance is to be undone fully. He must leave the mirror, confront the sordidness of the witch, subject himself to her blasphemous mumbo-jumbo[39] and drink the potion. That he does so and survives seems due to Mephistopheles's special intervention, since the witch expects the draught to kill him (2526-27). Mephistopheles will be less concerned to inhibit the fatal effects of the next potion that figures in the plot.

Faust is promised fast and powerful results; and the striking change in his manner and conduct when we next see him indicates that at least that promise was kept.

Straße

Since the end of *Studierzimmer II*, Faust has been dressed to match Mephistopheles's costume:

> In rotem, goldverbrämtem Kleide,
> Das Mäntelchen von starrer Seide,
> Die Hahnenfeder auf dem Hut,
> Mit einem langen, spitzen Degen (1536-39)

and now, magically made some thirty years younger, he has acquired the manner and bearing to match his garb. It is very much as a brash young nobleman sure of the charms of his person and his position that Faust accosts Gretchen; and she recognises the character of his approach at once. Calling her 'Fräulein', a title which her dress shows is not her due,[40] is a seducer's opening ploy. Gretchen's curt rejoinder that she is not a 'Fräulein' (that is, not of noble birth) is the appropriate rebuff. The brief exchange is in *Knittelvers*, as are the remainder of Faust's speeches in this scene. Though Faust's initial dis-

---

[39] Many scholars have determinedly sought elaborate and profound meanings in the goings-on of the witch and her simian entourage. For samples, see *39*, and the references given by Trunz (*1*), and Friedrich and Scheithauer (*23*) in their notes to this scene.

[40] Sumptuary laws requiring class differences to be plainly visible in clothing were still on the statute books in Goethe's day.

content was couched in this metre, it has never before been used for an expression of delight such as he now utters (2609-18). Partly, this establishes a rhythmic correspondence with Gretchen's reactions to the meeting (2678-2683); but it also helps to suggest that, at this stage, Faust's desires have as much to do with the aphrodisiac potion as they do with his familiar aspirations. As Mephistopheles gleefully points out, he is behaving like a stock figure of the randy man-about-town, and the uncouth metre suits his new identity.

Abend

Just as Gretchen's abruptness fascinated Faust rather than cooling his ardours, so too Faust's boldness has made an impression on Gretchen, though she seemed to scorn it. She is still thinking of him at the moment he is making his preparations to encounter her again.

The change that comes over Faust when he is left alone in Gretchen's room is marked by the departure from *Knittelvers*. Lines 2687-88 keep the four stresses, but with a wholly regular iambic metre, and the shift to the madrigal verse normally associated with Faust's expressions of longing is clearly made with the extra stresses in lines 2689-90. Faust as 'Hans Liederlich' has disappeared, as the rhythm of lines 2691-94 makes especially plain:

> Wie atmet rings Gefühl der Stille,
> Der Ordnung, der Zufriedenheit!
> In dieser Armut welche Fülle!
> In diesem Kerker welche Seligkeit!

Until the very end of line 2694, where 'Seligkeit', bringing an extra stressed syllable, marks the resumption of madrigal verse, this is the 'angelic' metre, heard in Faust's voice only once before, when he spoke of his sense of well-being at the start of *Studierzimmer I*. Then he felt for a moment part of a creation bound together by universal love: now he senses in the world

Gretchen inhabits a simple but intact order, with its own kind of blissful fulfilment available to those who are at home there.[41] Longing to be part of such a world, Faust 'throws himself' (stage direction preceding line 2695) into the armchair which he imagines was once a 'Väterthron' (2697) around which family festivities have been celebrated for many generations (2698-701), delighting in the aura of a secure patriarchal order, stable across time in its values and way of life.[42] And he feels that this spirit and Gretchen's spirit are one and the same.

Faust came here with the idea of procuring '... ein Halstuch von ihrer Brust, / Ein Strumpfband meiner Liebeslust!' (2661-62). The change within him is plain when the sight of Gretchen's bed, far from exciting lascivious thoughts, fills him with awe and wonder at another facet of her 'spirit'. As well as a contented member of a stable moral and social order, Gretchen is a masterpiece of nature's handiwork. He pictures her as a sleeping child through whose growth nature 'wove' in material substance the divine image of perfection she now represents (2711-16).

Everything Faust here so reverently evokes, he will help destroy. He will set Gretchen at odds with the only world she knows; and in the end he will bear the blame when nature's gentle handiwork is violently undone by the executioner's axe. That it is through his intuitions, so compellingly expressed, that we are made to feel the worth of what he shatters makes his offence all the greater. This is where Faust's acquisition of guilt, his descent into unquestionable evil, begins; and although Mephistopheles has provided the circumstances in which Faust's guilt is possible, Faust remains a free moral agent, wholly

[41] The metaphorical vocabulary Faust uses to evoke this simplicity can lead the unwary into misconceptions about Gretchen's social standing. She belongs to the reasonably comfortable urban lower middle-class. Though her father is dead, he left his widow and daughter securely provided for (3115-18). They live frugally out of thrift, not indigence, as the mother's practice of money-lending (2786-87) makes clear. So Faust's reference to her house as a 'Hütte' is no more an architectural description than the 'Kerker' of line 2694.

[42] But this stability does not mean that Faust is delighting in 'the eternal constants in human relationships', so that Gretchen becomes 'a symbol of timeless human experience' (*6*, pp.70-71). On the contrary, the whole appeal of this image to Faust lies in its vulnerability to precisely the kind of historical change which his way of life embodies.

responsible for the decision he takes.

The complexity of the moral issues raised by this scene has seldom been recognised. Most critics see in Faust's transition from lust to love an unambiguous moral advance. Admittedly, to view Gretchen simply as a sexual object is morally inferior to seeing her as a person. But to see someone as a person is not in itself a moral achievement: it merely opens up a new set of moral possibilities, for the worse as well as for the better. At this point, Faust becomes aware of those possibilities, and of the need to choose among them. Fully informed, knowing what he is doing, and for motives which are far from despicable, he chooses wrongly. Faust's perception of Gretchen as a person entails seeing how her whole being is rooted in a self-contained social, moral and religious order. That order has impinged upon Faust's life once before, on Easter Eve, but he knew that he could have no part in it. But that means he cannot enter Gretchen's life without tearing her out of what Mephistopheles mockingly calls her 'Dunstkreis' (2671), but which is as essential to her as the literal atmosphere she breathes. Gretchen, knowing nothing outside her own world, cannot conceive of her own vulnerability; but Faust can. A Faust as heartless seducer with no special understanding of what Gretchen is like and the sources from which she draws her vitality and composure would have a clear and measurable degree of guilt. (And a Gretchen who fell victim to such a Faust, though she would suffer pain and loss, would do so within a framework of values which still bound her to her familiar world and hence left her ability to make sense of her experience intact.) But the guilt of the Faust Goethe portrays, who sees and delights in what Gretchen is, yet in his quest for experience embarks on a course that can only destroy her, is immeasurably greater.

This is a guilt acquired in full knowledge, revealed by the decisive question in line 2719: 'Was willst du hier?' In asking himself this Faust is not contrasting his new awe towards Gretchen's person with his original seducer's intentions. He has done that in his first question, 'Was hat dich hergeführt?' (2717). He is now asking what he is doing here precisely as someone who grasps the gulf between Gretchen's world and his, who understands that the right response to the kind of love he now feels would be to pass up this experience and spare Gretchen an embroilment which can in the end only draw her out of the one medium in which she can exist. And he is capable, for a moment, of that right response. When Mephistopheles enters to warn of Gretchen's imminent return, Faust declares he will never come back (2730). As in the *Kerker* scene, everything hangs upon a swift departure; and, here too, Mephistopheles is at hand to prompt the wrong course. Where he later tries to hurry Faust and Gretchen into a flight together that would deprive Gretchen of her last spiritual refuge, he now induces Faust not to go without leaving behind the jewels which will ensure his return. At the end, Gretchen resists in a triumph of her remaining better judgement: Faust here abandons his moral sense and succumbs (2731-52).

The scene ends as it began with Gretchen alone, but aware that the atmosphere has somehow been defiled (2753-58). This is the first indication of that penetrating moral intuition which Gretchen will show more extensively later. To ward off her unease she sings a ballad, an example of Goethe's incomparable ability to blend the simplicity of folk poetry with self-effacing but consummate artistry. *Der König in Thule* is a song about keeping faith, both with a loved one who is dead, and with life, without which there could be no love. The deathbed gift is a goblet from which to drink 'Lebensglut': through this token the king's love outlasts death without turning away from life. The central image is of 'der alte Zecher' carousing as merrily as ever, though his eyes brim with tears at the memories his goblet holds. He bids farewell to the life he has enjoyed and the memory of his loss in a final energetic yet dignified gesture, draining the goblet one last time then casting it into the waves. The ballad evokes a fidelity that conquers time as fully as human mortality allows, drawing its strength not from contract or convention, but from love alone. Such fidelity can exist within all kinds of moral and religious schemes, but it is not dependent on any of them: it stands or falls with the personal qualities of the lovers. Gretchen, we may surmise, would be capable of it; Faust, to Gretchen's cost even more than his own, is not.

As Gretchen comes upon the jewels that will keep her thoughts on Faust, the *Knittelvers* characteristic of her speech shows (in the extra stresses of lines 2783 and 2785) a touch of the madrigal verse rhythm we associate with Faust and Mephistopheles: the subversive power of the intrusion into her life is signalled in rhythm as well as sense.

Spaziergang

The anecdote about how the jewels were 'swallowed' by the Church is a humorous foil to a serious matter: the fact that the die was cast in the previous scene when Faust left the jewels behind. By now, Faust shows no trace of hesitation and is urging Mephistopheles on as fiercely as he did in *Straße*: and Gretchen, we learn, 'Denkt ans Geschmeide Tag und Nacht, / Noch mehr an den, der's ihr gebracht' (2851). There is no going back for either of them now.

Der Nachbarin Haus

Knittelvers is employed again for the earthiness of Marthe, the would-be merry widow. Gretchen has entered into complicity with Marthe behind her mother's back: the second gift of jewels has had its insidious effect on her powers of judgement, despite her feelings that 'Es geht nicht zu mit rechten Dingen!' (2894).

Straße II

This scene concerns two oaths: the false one Faust is to swear about the death of Marthe's husband: and the protestations of love and fidelity that Faust will make to Gretchen. Mephistopheles insists they are essentially similar: why should Faust hesitate to make a false statement to Marthe when he will soon be lying to Gretchen as part of his seducer's role? The exchange that ensues needs careful scrutiny. Will not Faust soon, Mephistopheles asks, be swearing to Gretchen that he loves her? Yes, says Faust, and the words will come from the bottom of his heart. All right, says Mephistopheles; but will he not also be talking about the duration and fidelity of his love:

> Dan wird von ewiger Treu und Liebe,
> Von einzig überallmächt'gem Triebe —
> Wird das auch so von Herzen gehn? (3056-58)

Faust's reply, like his more famous answer to the 'Gretchen-frage', which it resembles stylistically, is a combination of impassioned intensity and rank equivocation. The lyrical outburst is in one sense a mask for the less exalted but more candid ploy of saying 'it all depends what you mean by ...'. All Faust is in effect saying is that the promises he will make to Gretchen will have powerful feelings behind them:

> Laß das! Es wird! — Wenn ich empfinde,
> Für das Gefühl, für das Gewühl
> Nach Namen suche, keinen finde,
> Dann durch die Welt mit allen Sinnen schweife,
> Nach allen höchsten Worten greife
> Und diese Glut, von der ich brenne,
> Unendlich, ewig, ewig nenne,
> Ist das ein teuflisch Lügenspiel? (3059-66)

Mephistopheles's reply hits the nail on the head: 'Ich hab doch recht!' What Faust has just said, despite — or even perhaps because of — his sincerity, proves Mephistopheles's point. When Faust swears eternal love to Gretchen, he will be using 'eternal' in his own way. And whatever there is to be said for that use, it is not what Gretchen will understand by the word. Such redefinitions of eternity in terms of quality rather than duration of experience are central to all secularisation of religious language; but the issue here, as Mephistopheles sees clearly enough, is not the meaning of words but the meaning of promises. The first is a matter for a dictionary, the second presupposes certain shared values and expectations. In giving a promise it is dishonest to use language in a sense — however well founded and defensible — different from the one in which the recipient understands it. And that is precisely what Faust is proposing to do, for there can be no question of Gretchen understanding eternity in anything other than its traditional sense of endless duration. Faust shrugs off the insight Mephistopheles has offered him by claiming it is pointless to bandy words with someone who is determined to be right (3069-70). More likely, he senses it is ill-advised to argue an indefensible position which it suits him to retain. We remember this is the same Faust who mocked Mephistopheles's wish to bind him by a formal agreement with the rejoinder that promises had no place in his view of a pervasively dynamic world: 'Rast nicht die Welt in allen Strömen fort, / Und mich soll ein Versprechen halten?' (1720-21). That rings truer to Faust's character and outlook than his words here, so Mephistopheles's glee is well-founded as he scents trouble ahead.

Garten — Ein Gartenhäuschen

Gretchen is here showing off, sprinkling her speech with Fremdwörter and inviting Faust to admire her sisterly devotion and frugal industry. And she is not without guile when she interrogates the flower in Faust's hearing, provoking just the response she hopes for, while unwittingly prefiguring her own undoing.[43] Gretchen is no saint. If she were, Faust would not see in her what he does, nor would she be affected by him as she is. She could not be at all exceptional without losing that complete accommodation to her world and its values which is the source of her attractiveness to Faust and the basis of her vulnerability.

Again Mephistopheles provides a humour which has its sinister side. We enjoy his tongue-in-cheek courting of Marthe, judging that she deserves no better; but though our first reaction is to see Faust's wooing of Gretchen as a contrast, Mephistopheles, in the preceding scene, has indicated that it, too, involves deception. The real difference is not between sincerity and stratagem, but between Faust the self-deceived deceiver and a Mephistopheles who knows exactly what he is doing.

In his confession of love, Faust makes an issue of what 'ewig' means:

---

[43] On the extent of that prefigurement, see *44*, pp.77-81.

> Laß diesen Händedruck dir sagen,
> Was unaussprechlich ist:
> Sich hinzugeben und eine Wonne
> Zu fühlen, die ewig sein muß!
> Ewig! — Ihr Ende würde Verzweiflung sein.
> Nein, kein Ende! Kein Ende! (3189-94)

This can hardly be for Gretchen's benefit. It is himself that Faust is reassuring as he insists that eternity as he understands it includes infinite duration as well as inexpressible intensity, despite Mephistopheles's taunts in the preceding scene. The reassurance may not be quite successful, which would suggest what passes through his mind in the moment of preoccupation (stage direction after line 3194) before he follows Gretchen into the summerhouse.

Gretchen's closing lines of *Knittelvers* (3211-16) with the especially homely rhyme of 'Kind' and 'find't', have more than a trace of the disingenuous about them. She was not, after all, the wholly passive recipient of Faust's advances, and she obviously takes delight in the fact that he does indeed 'see something in her'. But the slightly coy claim of 'Unwissenheit' is truer than she knows.

Wald und Höhle

The metre of the first part of this scene (3217-50) is the strongly run-on blank verse which is the normal medium of Goethe's classical plays, though it occurs nowhere else in *Faust I*.

After the preceding scene, it may be something of a surprise to find Faust, not speaking directly of his love for Gretchen, but extolling a new-found sense of closeness to nature and acknowledging it as the fulfilment of his request to the Erdgeist. He has been granted a revelation that his inmost self and the world he sees around him are part of a single dynamic order. He has come to know nature as one knows another person, instead of being confined to what he calls 'kalt staunenden Besuch' (3222). The contrast is not with an indifference to nature such as

Wagner showed in *Vor dem Tor* ('Man sieht sich leicht an Wald und Feldern satt' (1102)) but with Faust's former perception of nature as an object of the awe and fascination inspired by something beyond or above human grasp. Someone on a 'visit' is, by definition, away from home. But Faust now feels that nature is his true home, where he is welcomed and cherished by a motherly spirit.

But this is not yet the fulfilment of Faust's yearnings, because what he here describes as the Erdgeist's 'gifts' have included something unasked for, and yet in some sense inevitable: Mephistopheles,

> ... den Gefährten, den ich schon nicht mehr
> Entbehren kann, wenn er gleich, kalt und frech,
> Mich vor mir selbst erniedrigt, und zu Nichts,
> Mit einem Worthauch, deine Gaben wandelt.
>
> (3243-46)

Two roles of Mephistopheles are involved here. He provides the magic means to recover for Faust the youth which, in the course of nature, was gone for good: that is why he is Faust's 'indispensible' companion in his new-found vitality; and he embodies the power of reflective intelligence to debunk spontaneous experience, a power strongly present in Faust himself and which Mephistopheles never allows him to supress for long. Faust's complaint is not that Mephistopheles deflates what Faust values, but that Faust, with part of his mind, cannot deny the plausibility of what Mephistopheles says. When Mephistopheles's breath withers them, the Erdgeist's gifts turn to nothing in Faust's eyes too.

The closing lines of this passage (3249-50) betray the original placing of this scene after the seduction of Gretchen in *Faust: ein Fragment*. It is not so easy to see the sense of this couplet in the position which the scene finally came to occupy. But this defect, such as it is, counts for nothing against the dramatic force Goethe has given the scene by moving it forward. It now contains the very moment at which, spurred on by Mephistopheles, Faust resolves upon the final step to Gretchen's destruction, making the link between Faust's enjoyment of the Erdgeist's gifts and the evil to which Mephistopheles tempts him clear beyond all doubt.[44]

Faust's guilt towards Gretchen is underlined once more by lines 3345-65. He brings explicitly to mind what was already implied in his hesitation in Gretchen's room. He is 'der Flüchtling', 'der Unbehauste' (3348), the rootless modern intellectual, acknowledging no other authority than the unpredictable demands of his own self-development, yet nostalgic for the security enjoyed by those whose lives are still shaped by a traditional order. Faust compares himself to a raging torrent, and Gretchen to a peaceful dweller on its banks, seemingly safely held within her 'little world', who is taken unawares and swept to destruction:

> Und ich, der Gottverhaßte,
> Hatte nicht genug,
> Daß ich die Felsen faßte
> Und sie zu Trümmern schlug!
> Sie, ihren Frieden, mußt' ich untergraben!
>
> (3356-60)

Faust's awareness — and evasion — of moral responsibility is visible in the way he uses the word 'müssen'. In 'Sie, ihren Freiden, mußt' ich untergraben!' it is the idiomatic sense of 'müssen' implying reproach and therefore responsibility, as found also in English phrases like 'why did you have to do that?', where the actual meaning ('you need not have done that, yet you did') is virtually the opposite of the literal sense. In the next line this idiomatic 'müssen' of self-reproach, indicating a recognition of moral freedom, has been turned away from Faust himself, and is already shifting towards the literal 'müssen' of inevitability: 'Du, Hölle, mußtest dieses Opfer haben!'. And the

[44] Friedrich and Scheithauer show a trivial notion of how and when Faust acquires guilt when they claim that Goethe moved this scene forward 'offenbar weil das Selbstgespräch mit der feierlich-friedlichen Stimmung im Munde des noch nicht schuldigen Faust verständlicher erschien' (*23*, p.197). This also shows the equally common tendency among *Faust* interpreters to take the opening lines (3217-50) as a separable unit of meaning, as though they were not deliberately joined with what follows.

shift is complete when Faust proclaims, two lines further on, 'Was muß geschehn, mag's gleich geschehn!', using the 'müssen' of impersonal inevitability to disclaim responsibility for his own actions and their consequences. Having thus cast off his sense of freedom, his final move is to offer himself the dubious consolation of wishing that, if Gretchen 'must' be destroyed, her destruction may encompass his own: 'Mag ihr Geschick auf mich zusammenstürzen / Und sie mit mir zugrunde gehn!' (3364-65), as though such assent to his own downfall gave him the right to wreak havoc upon another person he claims to love.

At this point the two perspectives from which the action of the drama is perceived, the cosmic and the earthbound, come together for a moment into a single vision of evil, as Faust, without deviating from that pursuit of a fuller existence which makes him Der Herr's 'servant', nonetheless aligns himself with the powers of destruction. The fundamental issue that divides Mephistopheles from Der Herr, setting him in opposition to the divine goodness, is the relative value of being and non-being. But the worth of being as such cannot be separated from the worth of specific beings; and recognising the value of individual human beings involves not just an appreciation of their aesthetic or symbolic worth (such as Faust undeniably shows towards Gretchen), but also a respect for their intrinsic autonomy and value as persons, irrespective of any end which they may serve. In this decisive scene, Faust openly and deliberately subordinates Gretchen's existence to the cause of his own fulfilment, and in so doing enters into full alliance with the forces of negation. She is once again an object to be disposed of in his own interests, just as she was after his first encounter with her in the street. No longer simply a sexual object, admittedly, but nonetheless he is viewing her as the raw material of an experience that he 'must' have, whatever the cost to her. His unsavoury and implausible hope that her downfall will hurt him as much as it hurts her is only a sop to his conscience. Of Mephistopheles's many true remarks in the play, none is more apt than his comment, at the conclusion of this scene, that Faust is 'ziemlich eingeteufelt' (3371).

Gretchens Stube

The song Goethe here gives Gretchen, like *Der König in Thule*, another triumph of expressive simplicity gained through sophisticated means, lays bare Gretchen's vulnerability. She is now far past the stage of feeling flattered by Faust's attentions and is plainly in the grip of a passionate desire for him. Gretchen is no Victorian innocent. She knows perfectly well what Faust wants, and she wants it too, as this song makes abundantly clear. But unlike Faust, she has no inkling of what will become of her when his passion is spent, for the sheer strength of her feelings sweeps all thoughts other than her longing for him from her mind.

Marthens Garten

To grasp the considerable dramatic force of this scene we must attend to the acuteness of Gretchen's perceptions underneath her diffidence and apparent naivety. In putting what has become known as the 'Gretchenfrage' to Faust, 'wie hast du's mit der Religion?' (3415) she is not fundamentally concerned, as Faust would like to think, with whether he assents to religious dogmas. She is trying to explore and allay in the only terms available to her a well-founded fear that Faust belongs to a different moral world to her own. The beliefs she is really worried about are to do with the acceptance of certain cardinal values and priorities.

Faust immediately adopts the patronising tone he will keep throughout the scene:

> Laß das, mein Kind! Du fühlst, ich bin dir gut;
> Für meine Lieben ließ' ich Leib und Blut,
> Will niemand sein Gefühl und seine Kirche rauben.
>
> (3418-20)

We might wonder in passing just who these 'Lieben' for whom Faust would make such sacrifices are. They can hardly include Gretchen, since we have just seen Faust assent to her destruction in the cause of his own quest for experience; and anyway, the real issue is not any threat to Gretchen's beliefs, but of her intuition of a moral gulf between herself and Faust. Her query 'Glaubst du an Gott?' (3426) receives an answer (3431-58) which has often been admired as a fervently eloquent proclamation of pantheism.[45] What has less often been noted is that, as an answer to this question by this questioner, it is a good deal less than honest. Faust makes his notion of divinity plain enough for a sophisticated hearer (a notion that makes faith in Gretchen's sense meaningless, hence the claim that no one 'dare' affirm or deny belief in God as Faust understands him). But Gretchen is not intellectually sophisticated, and cannot catch the heterodoxy of Faust's confession: she hears only the echoes of familiar orthodox statements of divine ineffability: 'Ungefähr sagt das der Pfarrer auch, / Nur mit ein bißchen andern Worten' (3460-61). Perhaps Faust smiles inwardly at this remark; but we join him at our peril, for he is making the intellectual's cardinal error of confusing simplicity with simple-mindedness.

Gretchen is not to be shaken in her perception that there is something wrong with Faust, and her doggedness brings her steadily closer to the mark. Faust may have talked her into accepting that he is a believer of sorts, but that is not what really matters to Gretchen: 'Steht aber doch immer schief darum; / Denn du hast kein Christentum' (3467-68). This is awkwardly put, and we may at first miss the point; but when she expands upon the remark, we realise she is concerned about something essential: 'Der Mensch, den du da bei dir hast, / Ist mir in tiefer innrer Seele verhaßt' (3471-72). She is uneasy about Faust because she is uneasy about Mephistopheles. A new note of firmness and clarity appears in Gretchen's voice: this is something she is quite sure about, where she will not bow to Faust's supposedly superior knowledge. The force behind the second of those lines is demonstrated if we remove the 'innrer' and convert it to a line of normal (i.e. four-stress) *Knittelvers*. The extra emphasis which this additional stress gives every word in the line is the acoustic equivalent of Gretchen's intensity of conviction. In sound as well as sense, Faust's replies are far too light; and Gretchen, who was relatively easily placated by Faust's earlier

[45] For a fine analysis, see *45*.

responses, refuses to be put off.

Faust has now taken over the Mephistophelean role of trivialising evil — a sign of how well Mephistopheles's jocularity has won him over and of his deafness to the sinister undertones in that diabolical *bonhomie*. Gretchen makes no claims to special perceptiveness, indeed a chief cause of her disquiet is that it is Faust who is being strangely imperceptive about his companion:

> Man sieht, daß er an nichts keinen Anteil nimmt;
> Es steht ihm an der Stirn geschrieben,
> Daß er nicht mag eine Seele lieben. (3488-90)

The 'man sieht', and the 'es steht ihm an der Stirn geschrieben' emphasise the general obviousness of what Gretchen is talking about.

At this point the only hint of supernatural uncanniness is in line 3498: 'Auch, wenn er da ist, könnt' ich nimmer beten.' That apart, Mephistopheles is to Gretchen simply 'der Mensch, den du da bei dir hast', and it is as a sinister human being, sinister because of his lack of warmth and of love, that Gretchen fears him. As Faust's patronising trivialisation of Gretchen's disquiet continues, so the intensity of her feeling increases, until she makes her most extreme statement of the effect Mephistopheles has upon her:

> Das übermannt mich so sehr,
> Daß, wo er nur mag zu uns treten,
> Mein ich sogar, ich liebte dich nicht mehr.
>
> (3495-97)

What more could Gretchen say to bring home to Faust that her intuition cannot be lightly dismissed, especially when she implies that his readiness to dismiss it is the deepest source of her fears: 'Und das frißt mir ins Herz hinein; / Dir, Heinrich, muß es auch so sein' (3499-500)? But Faust refuses to take what she says seriously.[46] The man who thought himself a match for the

---

[46] Trunz takes a different view, which gives us a different Faust. According to his commentary on this scene (*1*, p.523), 'Gretchens Frage kommt aus tiefster

Erdgeist is put in the shade by the straightforward moral and psychological perceptiveness of a simple girl.

Faust produces a potion that will allow him to spend the night with Gretchen despite her mother's vigilance. She fears (correctly) that it may be harmful; Faust, sincerely no doubt but wrongly, assures her it is harmless. She takes his word on a matter of fact, though she could not take his reassurances on a matter of feeling. Love overcomes her better judgement; and from this moment she is wholly lost.

Am Brunnen

With stunning effect Goethe takes us straight from Mephistopheles's lewd gloating at the prospect of Faust's first secret assignation with Gretchen (3541-43) to two vignettes of a Gretchen who is already pregnant and fearing abandonment and disgrace.

The first is in *Knittelvers*, up to now the everyday medium of Gretchen's speech. She is fetching water from the well, an archetypal activity of a community still securely embedded in a 'patriarchal' way of life. Gossiping with another girl is all part of the everyday pattern. But this time the gossip has a chilling significance for Gretchen: it anticipates her own imminent exclusion from the community to which she still outwardly belongs. She cannot avoid disgrace any more than the unfortunate Bärbelchen, who, however her lover may behave, will not escape public humiliation. Gretchen realises she is now

Besorgnis. Faust erkennt das. Als er über Mephistopheles spricht, weiß er, daß er Phrasen macht'. This interpretation deprives the scene of much of its dramatic force, for it makes Gretchen the victim of a despicable character who knows her fears are well-founded, but callously fobs her off with trite rejoinders for his own convenience. But this would not be a clash between two perceptions, with Gretchen gaining in our eyes because of what she sees, and Faust losing because of what he cannot see (where his imperceptiveness is all of a piece with his general attitude to Mephistopheles and has been fostered by Mephistopheles's strategies). If Trunz were consistent here, he would have to suspect that Faust's assurances that the potion is harmless are a deliberate deception. Fortunately, there is no reason to see such a contemptible Faust in this scene. He gives Mephistopheles his own explanation for Gretchen's anxiety in 3528-33: she is worried that Faust may be damned for heterodoxy. Had he grasped the force of what Gretchen was saying about Mephistopheles, here would have been the moment to fling that in Mephistopheles's face, since Faust is so furious with him.

on the other side of a barrier she never imagined herself crossing; and she cannot grasp how such an experience as hers can have brought her there. Lieschen's catty account of how Bärbelchen came to grief (3551-60) assumes she is paying the price of straightforwardly shameful behaviour, an assumption Gretchen had herself once unthinkingly shared, along with everyone else she knew (3577-82). But Gretchen can see nothing in her own past that could justify what will happen to her: 'Doch — alles, was dazu mich trieb, / Gott! war so gut! ach, war so lieb!' (3585-86). Gretchen's intuitive self-judgement is at odds with the verdict demanded by the only system of values she knows: the seeds of derangement are sown. As Faust so correctly foresaw, Gretchen simply cannot cope with the effect which her encounter with him has on her life.

Zwinger

Gretchen's prayer of solitary anguish offers a different aspect of the same plight. The scene is in madrigal verse, the first time Gretchen's speech is consistently couched in this metre. If the exchange by the well foreshadowed Gretchen's public disgrace, her supplication to the Virgin Mary in the 'Zwinger' anticipates the path Gretchen will find out of the adversity which awaits her. Gretchen's alienation from the only world she knows will be not quite complete, for she will still find sustenance in the religious beliefs which, though part of that world, have a power that survives her social exclusion. It is important that the statue before which Gretchen prays is of the Mater Dolorosa, Mary afflicted by witnessing her son 'despised and rejected of men', not the triumphant Queen of Heaven. Still within the framework of her traditional outlook, Gretchen draws inspiration from this image in which solitude and rejection are acknowledged and transcended through faith in a divine compassion and mercy that overturns human cruelty and condemnation (3590-95). For the moment, Gretchen prays to be spared the coming torments, as did Christ in his solitary agony (3616). But the religious hope she is here evoking is for the transcendence of suffering, not its evasion. This prayer will not be answered in the way Gretchen wishes; but a kind of salvation will be granted her nonetheless through her faith. Goethe found the emphasis on Christ's sufferings in Western Christianity profoundly distasteful: it is a measure of his power and generosity of imagination that he could portray Gretchen's religious convictions with such sensitivity and a sympathy free of any hint of condescension.

Nacht. Straße vor Gretchens Türe

Through the death of Valentin, the breaking of the familial and social ties which held Gretchen securely in her world is enacted before our eyes.

Faust enters on his way to visit Gretchen; he is in a black mood which is powerfully conveyed, though not explained, by the image of a tiny sanctuary lamp threatened by encroaching gloom (3650-54). The enigmatic dejection encourages speculation. Perhaps the threatened light is his love for Gretchen. Is he now feeling the approach of that 'desperation' that he anticipated (3189-94) if his 'bliss' with her should prove finite, like everything else he has tried and found wanting? Mephistopheles is in gleeful high spirits. Remarking on the bright starlight, which will make him and Faust plainly visible (3678), he invites the attention of any curious neighbours by singing a questionable serenade outside Gretchen's window. Valentin's entry has established that the damage to Gretchen's reputation has already been done, but Mephistopheles is plainly not averse to making matters as bad as possible for her. He immediately seizes the opportunity of Valentin's emergence from the shadows to embroil Faust further. Valentin's courage is defeated by the cowardly blow which Faust strikes against the opponent whom magic has made defenceless.

Soldierly and blunt to the end, Valentin makes no fuss about his own death, sparing the last of his breath to castigate Gretchen, as the awakened neighbourhood listens, in the severest terms he can muster. His words may seem despicable; but he speaks 'als Soldat und brav' (3775) with the voice of his world, which is at its worst, from our modern perspective, in such situations where an individual has transgressed against the

social code. It is, after all, Gretchen's world as well, and what
Valentin embodies is simply the obverse side of that sense of
community which Faust so admired and envied. Lines 3772-73
epitomise the spirit of Valentin's life and death: 'Da du dich
sprachst der Ehre los, / Gabst mir den schwersten Herzensstoß.'
For Valentin, Gretchen and their neighbours there are no such
things as purely private transgressions. Not because everyone
pokes their noses into everybody else's business (which is
admittedly how it looks from a modern individualistic viewpoint), but because they know no distinction between public and
private matters. The way people judge themselves and those they
love accords completely with the way the community in which
they are embedded judges them. That is why Valentin's former
pride in his sister turns abruptly to self-contempt, as well as
contempt for her: her disgrace is a 'blow to the heart' from
which he cannot recover. We may not approve of this world; but
we can hardly condemn Valentin for living its life in the only
way he knows, nor does the scene invite us to. Again, Goethe's
generosity of imagination is striking.

Dom

This scene unites and intensifies the themes of *Am Brunnen*
and *Zwinger*. Gretchen is attempting to pray in a crowded
church at the public liturgy of the dead. The 'böser Geist' speaks
in her ear with the combined voices of self-reproach, public
blame and divine condemnation: there seems no solace from any
quarter. The spirit is 'evil', not because it reproaches her for the
deaths to which she has been a party, but because it tempts her
to despair of forgiveness (exactly the despair that finally damned
the *Faustbuch* figure). Here she succumbs and falls into a faint
before the *Dies Irae* being chanted in the background makes its
turn (at the verse 'Recordare Jesu pie...') from fear of divine
judgement towards the trust in divine compassion evoked in
Zwinger. But in the final scene, casting herself upon God's
judgement, she will put this spirit, as well as Faust and
Mephistopheles, truly behind her once and for all.

Walpurgisnacht. Walpurgisnachtstraum

It is hard to endorse the view that the *Walpurgisnacht* and the *Walpurgisnachtstraum* which follows it form one of the 'high points' (*30*, p.88) of the play. Certainly, the scenes are rich in motifs to be traced, structures to be elucidated and allusions to be explicated; and there is also the body of material presented by Schöne (*40*) which, for one reason or another, did not find its way into the published version, and which can foster speculation about a different *Walpurgisnacht* that would have been part of a substantially different play. But allusions, leitmotifs and tantalising omissions do not in themselves make for literary quality, especially in drama, and there is much in these scenes that is thin and tedious.

The beginning is as powerful as anything else in the work. Faust and Mephistopheles ascend the Brocken, presumably late in the evening. For Faust, this is an envigorating walk, one of whose chief pleasures is to feel the rebirth of the new year (3845-47). In lines 3848-55 there follows a characteristically Mephistophelean deflation of the same scene. The contrasting attitudes remind us of Faust's walk with Wagner the previous spring; but Faust is about to be introduced into company very different from the people he found *Vor dem Tor*, despite the common festival mood. Mephistopheles wants not the slow regenerative pace of nature, enjoyed through sustained human effort, but the magical unleashing of chaotic energies that awaits them further up the mountain. Once Mephistopheles has enlisted the aid of the will-o'-the-wisp, their course becomes unnaturally swift (3876-77); and soon the violence of their motion takes away all sense of direction (3906-07). Moreover, there is no longer a contrast of attitudes between identifiable figures, but a *Wechselgesang* involving man, devil and nature-spirit in which all share an increasing sense of bewilderment mingled with intoxication as the surroundings, and the company, become more and more uncanny, less and less like the customary sights and sounds of nature on a mountain. This transformation from the natural to the eerie culminates in Faust's description of the emerging glow of Mammon (3916-31), after which the literary quality of the scene deteriorates.

Goethe doubtless knew that the victims of witch hunts, pressed under torture to identify people they had seen at witches' sabbaths, often named their enemies. So it must have seemed a good idea to allow Faust, in his trip up the Brocken, to encounter various figures whose person or views Goethe himself disliked. There is, of course, no reason why literary, ideological or political satire should not be incorporated into a play of this kind. But to hold its own in the company of the other scenes, it would have to be rather better — sharper, more ferocious and aimed at more exacting targets — than what Goethe offers here. Nothing is more deservedly ephemeral than flat satire. The commentaries offer ample explication for readers curious to know why they are supposed to be amused.

More impressive and effective are the allusions to matters internal to the plot, especially the parallel Mephistopheles makes, as he leads Faust towards a group of witches, between this occasion and the encounter with Gretchen in Marthe's garden which he, too arranged: 'Ich tret heran und führe dich herein, / Und ich verbinde dich aufs neue' (4053-54). If, as Faust will later claim in his fury, this is all a 'distraction' designed to keep him in ignorance of Gretchen's fate, it shows that bitter truth hidden under deceptive frivolity which is so characteristic of Mephistopheles. For the very terms on which Mephistopheles offers the new 'distractions' should make Faust think of his old commitments, just as the wares hawked by the Trödelhexe (4096-109), the poisoned cup, the seductive jewelry, the sword that has been an instrument of cowardly murder, should remind him of his misdeeds; and Mephistopheles's insistence that such things are 'out of date' (4110-13) should strike Faust as all too obviously false, a plain instance of Mephistopheles mocking as *passé* notions of evil which he himself still exemplifies and puts into effect. But Faust, as with Gretchen's fears, seems to think this is all fairly harmless, if rather disorderly fun: 'Daß ich mich nur nicht selbst vergesse! / Heiß ich mir das doch eine Messe!' (4114-15).

It takes something much more obviously sinister to bring Faust out of his holiday mood: the vision of Gretchen beheaded

(4183-205). It is hard to see why so many critics think Mephistopheles's remarks about this figure are simply lies or evasions: there is ample truth in the warning

> Ihm zu begegnen, ist nicht gut:
> Vom starren Blick erstarrt des Menschen Blut,
> Und er wird fast in Stein verkehrt; (4191-93)

We shall soon see this happening to Faust when he encounters the real Gretchen in the predicament which this 'Idol' enacts. We do not hear of Faust again until he has made the discovery. Perhaps he is as little interested in the *Walpurgisnachtstraum* as is a modern audience.

Trüber Tag. Feld

From the fripperies of ghostly amateur theatricals, we pass at once to a scene of passionate fury as Faust curses Mephistopheles for letting him remain ignorant of Gretchen's plight. The chronology is odd. On the night of Valentin's death, when Gretchen was plainly still pregnant and at home, Mephistopheles spoke of 'Walpurgisnacht' as 'the day after tomorrow' (3661-62). So either Faust has had other protracted adventures after 'Walpurgisnacht', oblivious to Gretchen's plight despite the vision he saw there, or this scene's reference to Gretchen having wandered the earth in misery 'for a long time' makes no sense. There seems little point in making heavy weather of the matter: it would be of real importance only if Faust's guilt began with his abandoning or neglecting Gretchen. But the essence of his guilt is elsewhere, it arises much earlier in the play in circumstances portrayed with all the necessary clarity when he knowingly assents to a course of action which must, sooner or later, destroy her. The actual details of how the disaster which Faust's choices have made inevitable comes about are of comparatively little importance.

Of the prose scenes in the *Urfaust*, this is the only one that was not recast into verse for *Faust I*. Critics frequently suggest that Faust's anguish is too stark and overwhelming for the discipline of metre; yet the strongest impression made by Faust's speeches here is of declamatory rhetoric verging upon bombast, especially when set against the terse accuracy of Mephistopheles's rejoinders. Perhaps the concision of verse would have lent Faust's outbursts a weight which Goethe did not wish them to receive. No doubt Faust's feelings are intense and genuine; but he protests Mephistopheles's guilt and his own innocence rather too extravagantly to carry full conviction.

Mephistopheles's defence against the curses Faust flings at him is plausible enough: he coolly points out that Faust is now complaining about a price he was once willing to pay. Faust is brought to a new pitch of fury by Mephitopheles's 'Sie ist die erste nicht', hearing in this callous generalisation the antithesis of his own intense concern: 'Mir wühlt es Mark und Leben durch, das Elend dieser einzigen — du grinsest gelassen über das Schicksal von Tausenden hin!' Yet Faust himself foresaw misery for Gretchen, and assented, albeit with uneasy mind, to be its agent. Mephistopheles confronts him with the recognition that he is reaping the consequences of his own decision, including above all the decision to seek diabolical assistance: 'Warum machst du Gemeinschaft mit uns, wenn du sie nicht durchführen kannst?'. Finally Mephistopheles puts the question to which Faust has not answer other than a look of deranged fury: 'Wer war's, der sie ins Verderben stürzte? Ich oder du?'

Faust reacts to these home truths as if they were scandalous evasions. Like the corresponding complaint about Mephistopheles in *Wald und Höhle*, Faust's appeal to the Erdgeist ('warum an den Schandgesellen mich schmieden...') falsely implies that Mephistopheles was inflicted upon him against his will. The truth of the matter is in another of Mephistopheles's unanswerable questions, 'Drangen wir uns dir auf, oder du uns?', and Faust's actions belie his words as he demands Mephistopheles's magical services yet again, this time to free Gretchen. What kind of liberty that would be, Faust does not consider.

Nacht, offen Feld

Galloping on their diabolical steeds to reach Gretchen's prison
before dawn, Faust and Mephistopheles pass by the place of
execution. Mephistopheles claims ignorance of what the
mysterious figures they see there are doing; Faust sees their
gestures as an act of consecration. The preparations for
Gretchen's execution are proceeding, heedless of Faust's frantic
mission and presaging its failure. That failure will not, however,
be the work of an inexorable fate, but the consequence of
Gretchen's free rejection of what Faust is racing to offer her.

Kerker

There are obvious parallels between the opening of this scene
and *Abend*. Like Faust's first intrusion into Gretchen's world,
his arrival at her prison cell is effected surreptitiously and with
the aid of magic; and he is overcome on the threshold by 'ein
längst entwohnter Schauer' (4405) which recalls his
'Wonnegraus' on opening the curtain round Gretchen's bed.
Then, Faust spoke of Gretchen's room as a 'Kerker'
transformed by her presence into a heavenly domain. Now he
has helped bring her into a literal prison which she fears borders
upon hell itself (4454-59).

Gretchen's song both reveals and interprets her derangement.
It is sung by the child in the fairy-tale of the juniper tree, killed
by its stepmother but restored to life by its sister's love. We
recall Gretchen's pride in rearing her own infant sister (3121-43):
that child eventually died despite her care, now her own child
has died at her hand. Her mind is struggling with her mingled
sense of intense guilt and essential innocence. At one level she
suppresses the knowledge of what she has done, telling herself
that her baby has been stolen from her:

Sie singen Lieder auf mich! Es ist bös von den Leuten!
Ein altes Märchen endigt so,
Wer heißt sie's deuten? (4448-50)

'They' — all those who pass judgement upon her — are, she

feels, wrongly interpreting her role in the fairy-tale, making her the evil mother when she is sure she is the good sister.

Though Faust finds a Gretchen driven mad by guilt, confusion and despair, neither the perceptiveness which made her mistrust Mephistopheles nor the love for Faust which outweighed that mistrust are extinguished. Though she at first mistakes Faust for the executioner (4423-40), she recognises his voice when he abandons furtive speech and shouts her name (4460); and with the recognition comes a surge of joy which, for a moment, wipes out all memory of her immediate past (as the move to the present tense underlines):

> Schon ist die Straße wieder da,
> Auf der ich dich zum ersten Male sah,
> Und der heitere Garten,
> Wo ich und Marthe deiner warten. (4475-78)

The power of her love for Faust brings Gretchen to her senses; but that does not help Faust's plans for her rescue. Recapitulating in a few moments the course of their relationship, Gretchen sees in Faust's eagerness to be off a sudden coldness, the inexplicable death of his love (4493-97). And when she turns back to him, it is to put a question more penetrating than any she posed in Marthe's garden: 'Wie kommt es, daß du dich vor mir nicht scheust?— / Und weißt du denn, mein Freund, wen du befreist?' (4504-05).

More than anything else in this scene, this question makes plain that Gretchen is not simply afflicted, in the modish phrase, by 'guilt feelings': she has an ineradicable sense of moral responsibility. Just as earlier, Faust's association with Mephistopheles made her uneasy about his character, so now his eagerness to free her, when she does not, finally, believe she deserves freedom, alerts her to the moral gulf between them. If they do indeed belong together, it is in shared responsibility for deeds which she abhors, a thought which is hinted at in lines which movingly mingle all the elements — guilt, bewilderment, love, delight and revulsion — which make up Gretchen's feelings on seeing Faust again:

> Meine Mutter hab ich umgebracht,
> Mein Kind hab ich ertränkt.
> War es nicht dir und mir geschenkt?
> Dir auch — Du bist's! ich glaub es kaum.
> Gib deine Hand! Es ist kein Traum!
> Deine liebe Hand! — Ach, aber sie ist feucht!
> Wische sie ab! Wie mich deucht,
> Ist Blut daran. (4507-14)

The blood, of course, belongs to Valentin.

Faust's response to this powerful sense of shared guilt is perhaps the most chilling utterance in the entire play: 'Laß das Vergangne vergangen sein, / Du bringst mich um' (4518-19). This debases a shared personal 'Vergangenheit' which shapes present awareness and determines future plans into an impersonal 'das Vergangne'. For inappropriateness to the person and the situation, it rivals Mephistopheles's 'sie ist die erste nicht'. Gretchen makes no response. Her 'Nein!' at the start of line 4520 is a withdrawal of her suggestion that Faust should share her captivity and penalty: someone, she now decides, must live to tend the graves, hers included. Otherwise, there will be nobody to pay their respects to her mother or Valentin; and her grave, as a criminal's, will be shunned.

'Nur *einen* Schritt, so bist du frei!', Faust urges her (4564). But she cannot take that step, not because she is too insane to grasp what Faust is proposing, but because she rejects the only kind of freedom he can offer, where she would be a fugitive (4544-49), tormented by conscience and memory. She slips once more into hallucination, but what she sees — her child still thrashing in the water, her mother falling into the drugged sleep from which she never woke (4551-73) — are emblems of her guilt, her awareness that things which can neither be undone nor forgotten close off the path of freedom Faust wants her to follow.

Mephistopheles's intervention (4597) forces a conclusion. His appearance brings Gretchen a final clarity about what she cannot do and does not want. She grasps that to be saved through his assistance would be to be fetched by the devil, to escape physical destruction at the price of intolerable spiritual torment. She resolves to take her stand alone before divine justice, where she trusts for mercy if she faces her past, her self and her guilt; and in the moment of decisive resolution she no longer sees Mephistopheles as a mere associate whom Faust could 'send away' if he wished. Once, Gretchen contrasted her longing to see Faust with her horror of meeting Mephistopheles in his company: 'Aber wie ich mich sehne, dich zu schauen, / Hab ich vor dem Menschen ein heimlich Grauen' (3479-80). Now she invokes angelic protection, not just against Mephistopheles, but against Faust himself, who fills her with a horror greater than the ignominious death that awaits her: 'Heinrich! Mir graut's vor dir' (4610). With these words she assents to her death, recognising in the man she still loves the embodiment of the evil she abhors in the world and herself.

Four exclamations in rapid succession bring *Faust I* to an end. The first two, Mephistopheles's 'Sie ist gerichtet!', abandoning her to earthly condemnation, and the Stimme (*von oben*) which proclaims her vindication by a divine tribunal, have attracted a disproportionate amount of attention. Even more significant are the last two: Mephistopheles's 'Her zu mir!', recalling Faust to the diabolical company where Gretchen feels he now belongs; and the last utterance of the play, the sound of Gretchen's voice crying out Faust's name, echoing from her dungeon then dying away. So Gretchen's last word is not her outburst of revulsion but her devastating cry of abandoned, hopeless but undiminished love.

A Prospective Conclusion

The two final exclamations leave Faust's salvation very much in the balance as the play ends. Mephistopheles reclaims Faust and Faust obeys his call. From the cosmic perspective, the decisive question is not what Faust has done but what his response to it will be: will he continue to strive for ever fuller experience, remaining in that sense Der Herr's faithful servant, despite the havoc he has wrought? To do so, he would surely need to mingle a measure of Mephistopheles's detachment with his zest for experience; and that would be a 'gentle' step in the diabolical direction of just the kind Mephistopheles had in mind. (At the start of *Faust II*, Goethe does offer a solution to the problem of keeping Faust's striving alive without such contamination, but on terms so different from those in which *Faust I* poses the issue that it must be left aside here.) Faust's damnation, as the play understands it, seems from this aspect very much a possibility at the close of the play.

From the earthly perspective, what matters is the cost of Faust's quest to an innocent victim. Claims that Gretchen should feel honoured to be crushed by such a man as Faust, or grateful for an encounter that expands her horizons, though it unfortunately ruins her life, will not do. Only if the play gives us some vestigial sign that Gretchen can assent to her fate, not because it makes sense in her eyes or anyone else's, but simply because it was inflicted upon her by someone for whom she feels an inextinguishable love, is there any prospect of Faust escaping human condemnation. Her final cry may be just that sign.

At the end of *Faust II*, Faust is saved and Mephistopheles confounded; but hardly justly because, as is generally held, he has carried on striving to the last. The notion that Faust has *merited* salvation is denied by the concentration, in both parts of the play, on the dire consequences for others of his aspirations, furthered as they are by Mephistopheles's maliciously destructive assistance. The complex and elusive symbolism of the closing scene of *Faust II* cannot be summarised simply; but one important element which accounts for Faust's symbolic salvation is Gretchen's intercession on his behalf. In loving Faust to the end, despite the horror he inspires in her, she is holding fast to something which she cherishes despite the catastrophe, even though it is that catastrophe's root cause. No one, apart from Gretchen herself, has any right to discern value in her sufferings; but that she can, and does, retain her love for Faust in spite of everything wrenches from the apparently senseless destruction of her existence something whose worth is proof against Mephistopheles's cynicism, a counterweight to his claim that a world of creatures capable of inflicting such anguish upon one another should never have come into being. Gretchen's love for Faust, surviving the worst that can be known about him, persisting even beyond her conviction that she must sever her lot from his, is a secular analogue of Christian redemption, the psychological equivalent of the theology of wholly unmerited justification, a scandal to the wise precisely because it is granted in the face of the fullest conceivable awareness that it is undeserved.

Faust I was ushered in with Der Herr's confidence that Faust's future would vindicate the worth of human existence; it closes with a recognition that such vindication, if it can indeed be achieved by what is still to come, may be problematic and all but intolerably costly. The ending of *Faust II* will suggest that in a cosmic span the forces of destruction and negation do not triumph; but their power in the short term within which human lives are lived and lost, once and for all, has proved far greater and more harrowing than the serene confidence of Der Herr's heavenly viewpoint led us to anticipate. That austere insight, far less comfortable than anything Goethe's own talk about his conciliatory nature might prepare us for, means that no special pleading is required to justify the generic description chosen for the play by its author. No matter what final outcome we imagine for the Faust whom Mephistopheles whisks away from Gretchen's death cell, the sense that a tragedy has been enacted is inescapable.

That tragedy is not blunted by its origins in a particular historical transition. Living in history is not an avoidable accident, beneath the dignity of tragic art, but an essential part of the human condition. Gretchen, the innocent inhabitant of an older order, falls victim to the ethic of self-realisation which has been the glory and the curse of Western civilisation since the Enlightenment. Her death is as intolerable as the essential impulse behind Faust's striving is admirable. A story seemingly inseparable from a medieval world-view has been transformed, through Goethe's genius, into the tragedy *par excellence* of modernity.

Appendix

Some Rudiments of German Prosody

This is simply a rough outline of the bare minimum of knowledge needed to appreciate the versification in *Faust I*. For simplicity's sake, the important issue of different degrees of stress is ignored: all stressed syllables are treated alike, and marked in the quotations by ′ . ᵕ denotes an unstressed syllable.

Two highly readable books can supply some of the detail which this appendix overlooks or oversimplifies: Wolfgang Kayser, *Kleine deutsche Versschule* (Berne and Munich: Francke, 1946, many reprints); and Paul Fussel, *Poetic Meter and Poetic Form* (New York: Random House, revised edition, 1979). The latter, though about English verse, is still of great use to the reader of German, since the prosody of the two languages is very similar.

Unlike classical Latin or Greek verse, which is scanned by the length of the vowel sounds, and unlike French verse, where all syllables are counted, Geman verse is scanned by reference to the number of stressed syllables and their relation to the unstressed syllables which surround them. The term 'foot' has no precise significance in German scansion, but particular rhythmic patterns are named by loose analogy with classical 'feet':

Iambic verse consists of lines where each stressed syllable is preceded by a single unstressed one.

Trochaic verse (hardly employed in *Faust I*) has a stressed syllable beginning the line, with each stressed syllable followed by a single unstressed one.

Dactylic rhythm occurs where a stressed syllable is followed by two unstressed ones.

The *metre* of a given passage of verse is the pattern of stresses which we are led to expect when we read it: the actual *rhythm* of a given line may deviate from this metre to some degree (by reversing the expected positions of a stressed and unstressed syllable, for example).

To identify a metre, we need to know:

a) how many stressed syllables there are in a line,

and

b) how many unstressed syllables generally occur between them.

The main metres employed in *Faust I* are:

i) *Knittelvers*. In Goethe's usage, this consists of lines in which four stressed syllables are separated by a highly variable number of unstressed syllables. The lines invariably rhyme according to a simple scheme.

ii) Four-beat iambic. A single unstressed syllable precedes each of four stressed syllables. (Sometimes, an extra final unstressed syllable is supplied by a feminine rhyme, see below.) In common with all patterns where the number of intervening unstressed syllables is carefully controlled (in sharp contrast to *Knittelvers*), such metre is termed 'regular'.

iii) Madrigal verse. A difficult metre to specify, since the number of stressed syllables can vary from line to line. There are one or two (but hardly ever any more) unstressed syllables between the stresses. The lines are rhymed, and the pattern of rhyme may be quite elaborate.

iv) Blank verse. Five beat iambic lines, unrhymed.

v) Free rhythms. No identifiable regular pattern of stress. Line breaks determined by pattern of feeling or meaning. There may be sporadic rhymes, but no regular pattern.

Rhymes are classified according to whether the final syllable of the rhyming words is stressed (*masculine* rhyme) or unstressed (*feminine* rhyme). Adjacent pairs of rhyming lines are called rhyming couplets, while a pattern which rhymes alternate lines is called *Kreuzreim*.

Lines where the flow of sense pauses at the line ends are termed *end-stopped*: if *enjambement* carries the voice across the line-end in an unbroken flow, the lines are said to be *run on*.

Select Bibliography

ABBREVIATIONS FOR PERIODICALS AND SERIAL PUBLICATIONS

GLL	German Life and Letters
GQ	German Quarterly
JES	Journal of European Studies
LGS	London German Studies
OL	Orbis Litterarum
PEGS	Publications of the English Goethe Society

A. PRIMARY TEXTS

1. *Goethes Werke, Hamburger Ausgabe*, Vol.3, edited by E. Trunz, 11th edition (Munich: C.H. Beck, 1981).
2. Goethe, *Faust: der Tragödie erster Teil*, edited by L.J. Scheithauer (Stuttgart: Reclam, 1971).
3. ——, *Faust I*, edited by W.H. Bruford (London: Macmillan, 1968).
4. *Historia von Johann Fausten*, edited by R. Benz (Stuttgart: Reclam, 1972).

B. SECONDARY LITERATURE

5. M.H. Abrams, *Natural Supernaturalism* (New York: W.W. Norton, 1971).
6. S. Atkins, *Goethe's 'Faust': a literary analysis* (Cambridge, Mass.: Harvard University Press, 1958).
7. ——, 'Faustforschung und Faustdeutung seit 1945', *Euphorion*, 53 (1959), pp.422-40.
8. ——, 'The Interpretation of Goethe's *Faust* since 1958', *OL*, 20 (1965), pp.239-67.
9. E.A. Blackall, *The Emergence of German as a Literary Language* (Cambridge: University Press, 1959).
10. P. Boyde, *Dante, Philomythes and Philosopher: man in the cosmos* (Cambridge: University Press, 1981).
11. N. Boyle, 'Approaching *Faust I*', *JES*, 8 (1978), pp.175-202.
12. ——, '"Du ahnungsloser Engel, du!": some current views of Goethe's *Faust*', *GLL*, 36 (1982/3), pp.116-47.
13. W.H. Bruford, *Goethe's 'Faust I' Scene by Scene* (London: Macmillan, 1968). (Though unlisted in the British National Bibliography, and uncatalogued by the British Library or the Library of Congress, this book does exist!)

14. R. Buchwald, *Führer durch Goethes Faustdichtung*, 4th edition (Stuttgart: Kröner, 1955).

15. E.M. Butler, *The Myth of the Magus* (Cambridge: University Press, 1948).

16. ——, *Ritual Magic* (Cambridge: University Press, 1949).

17. ——, *The Fortunes of Faust* (Cambridge: University Press, 1952).

18. N. Cohn, *Europe's Inner Demons* (London: Heinemann, 1975).

19. L. Dieckmann, *Goethes 'Faust': a critical reading* (Englewood Cliffs, NJ: Prentice Hall, 1972).

20. O. Durrani, *Faust and the Bible* (Berne: Lang, 1977).

21. B. Fairley, *Goethe's 'Faust': six essays* (Oxford: University Press, 1953).

22. F.M. Fowler, 'Symmetry of structure in Goethe's *Faust, Part One*', *LGS*, 3 (1986), pp.22-40.

23. T. Friedrich and L.J. Scheithauer, *Kommentar zu Goethes 'Faust'* (Stuttgart: Reclam, 1974).

24. A. Gillies, *Goethes 'Faust': an interpretation* (Oxford: Blackwell, 1957).

25. U.K. Goldsmith, 'Ambiguity in Goethe's *Faust*: a lecture for the general reader', *GQ*, 39 (1966), pp.311-28.

26. R. Gray, *Goethe: a critical introduction* (Cambridge: University Press, 1968).

27. H. Haile, *Invitation to Goethe's 'Faust'* (Alabama: University Press, 1979).

28. H. Jantz, *The Form of 'Faust': the work of art and its intrinsic structures* (Baltimore: Johns Hopkins University Press, 1978).

29. W. Kayser, *Kunst und Spiel* (Göttingen: Vandenhoeck & Ruprecht, 1961), pp.86-99, 'Goethes Gedichte in Stanzen'.

30. H. Kobligk, *Goethe: 'Faust I'* (Frankfurt am Main: Diesterweg, 1978).

31. A.O. Lovejoy, *The Great Chain of Being* (Cambridge, Mass.: Harvard University Press, 1936).

32. G. Lukács, *Faust und Faustus* (Reinbeck bei Hamburg: Rowohlt, 1971).

33. G. Mahal, 'Der tausendjährige Faust: Rezeption als Anmassung', in *Literatur und Leser*, edited by G. Grimm (Stuttgart: Reclam, 1975), pp.181-95.

34. E.C. Mason, *Goethe's 'Faust': its genesis and purport* (Berkeley and Los Angeles: University of California Press, 1967).

35. V. Nollendorf, *Der Streit um den Urfaust* (The Hague: Mouton, 1967).

36. P. Pütz, 'Faust und der Erdgeist' in *Untersuchungen zur Literatur als Geschichte: Festschrift für Benno von Wiese*, edited by V.J. Günther, H. Koopmann, P. Pütz, H.J. Schrimpf (Berlin: Erich Schmidt, 1973), pp.171-81.

37. P. Requadt, *Goethes 'Faust I': Leitmotivik und Architektur* (Munich: Fink, 1972).

38. W. Resenhöfft, 'Die Widerspruchslosigkeit der Zeitrechnung von *Faust I*', *Goethe*, 32 (1970), pp.55-60.

39. ——, *Goethes Rätseldichtungen im 'Faust'* Berne: Lang, 1972).

40. A. Schöne, *Götterzeichen, Liebeszauber, Satanskult* (Munich: C.H. Beck, 1982).

41. H. Schwerte, *Faust und das Faustische; ein Kapitel deutscher Ideologie* (Stuttgart: Klett, 1962).

42. E. Staiger, *Goethe*, Vol.1 (Zurich: Atlantis, 1952) and Vol.2 (Zurich: Atlantis, 1956).

43. L. Trilling, *Sincerity and Authenticity* (London: Oxford University Press, 1974).

44. I.A. White, *Names and Nomenclature in Goethe's 'Faust'* (London: Institute of Germanic Studies, 1980).

45. E.M. Wilkinson, 'The Theological Basis of Faust's Credo', *GLL*, 10 (1956/7), pp.229-39.

46. E.M. Wilkinson and L.A. Willoughby, 'Glossary', in Schiller, *Über die ästhetische Erziehung des Menschen in einer Reihe von Briefen*, edited by E.M. Wilkinson and L.A. Willoughby (Oxford: Clarendon Press, 1967).

47. L.A. Willoughby, 'Goethe's *Faust*: a morphological approach', in E.M. Wilkinson and L.A. Willoughby, *Goethe: Poet and Thinker* (London: Barnes & Noble, 1962), pp.95-117.

48. M. Winkler, 'Zur Bedeutung der verschiedenen Versmaße von *Faust I*', *Symposium*, 18 (1964), pp.5-21.

49. W. Wittkowski, 'Gedenke zu Leben!: Schuld und Sorge in Goethes *Faust*', *PEGS*, 38 (1967/68), pp.114-45.

50. R.C. Zimmermann, *Das Weltbild des jungen Goethe* (Munich: Fink, 1969).